Recent Research in Psychology

Lawrence A. Ponemon David R.L. Gabhart
Editors

Auditing
Advances in Behavioral Research

With 16 Figures

Springer-Verlag
New York Berlin Heidelberg London Paris
Tokyo Hong Kong Barcelona Budapest

Lawrence A. Ponemon
Mueller Chair of Accounting Research
Division of Accounting and Law
School of Management
Babson College
Babson Park, MA 02157-0901
USA

David R. L. Gabhart
Department of Accountancy
Bentley College
Waltham, MA 02254-4705
USA

Library of Congress Cataloging-in-Publication Data
Auditing : advances in behavioral research / Lawrence A. Ponemon, David R.L. Gabhart, editors.
p. cm. — (Recent research in psychology)
Includes bibliographical references.
ISBN-13:978-0-387-97619-8 e-ISBN-13:978-1-4612-3190-5

DOI: 10.1007/978-1-4612-3190-5

1. Auditing—Research. 2. Experimental research. I. Ponemon, Lawrence A. II. Gabhart, David R.L. III. Series.
HF5667.E97 1992
657'.45—dc20 91-28840

Printed on acid-free paper.

Softcover reprint of the hardcover 1st edition 1991

Camera ready copy provided by the authors.

9 8 7 6 5 4 3 2 1

ISBN-13:978-0-387-97619-8 Springer-Verlag New York Berlin Heidelberg
e-ISBN-13:978-1-4612-3190-5 Springer-Verlag Berlin Heidelberg New York

Preface

This book has been prepared for those readers who want to maintain their knowledge of current developments in the field of behavioral research as applied to auditing. The articles and papers presented in this volume were selected because they will contribute to the knowledge and advancement of not only the individual researcher or educator, but also of the profession.

It is our belief that if research endeavors may be viewed as having stages of life, then the field of behavioral research in auditing is in its genesis. Almost twenty years ago, in speaking of the state of the art of psychology, William Hays expressed a most appropriate thought:

> Experimental evidence is accumulating at a rapid rate in psychology, and efforts at constructing psychological theories with mathematical deductive power are constantly being made. However, it seems safe to say that it will be sometime before there are psychological laws and theories on a par with those of physics. The absence of a general theory does not imply that those relations are missing or unimportant in psychology; the discovery and specification of relations is the process by which those theories are built. (Hays, 1973, p. 40.)

In the first chapter, "Experimental Research and the Distinctive Features of Accounting Settings," Robert Libby presents an encompassing and knowledgeable summary of the changes that have taken place during the last decade in human information processing research in accounting and experimental economics as it relates to those issues.

In "Reconsidering the Definition of Structure as it Relates to Differentiation Among Public Accounting Firms," Wanda Wallace looks at the problem of an aggregate metric that differentiates public accounting firms based on the degree to which their approaches tend to be structured and suggests means of disaggregating that metric. She proposes disaggregating structure along the lines of individual staff, office management, national management, and the decision process relevant to the task at hand so that a better understanding of structure could evolve.

While many researchers have concentrated on the accuracy of audit judgments, Urton Anderson, Lisa Koonce, and Garry Marchant investigate the cognitive processes by which auditors make their judgments in "A Model of Audit Judgment: Cognition In A Professional Context." The authors posit a mental model of the basic reasoning skills used in the context of professional audit judgment.

One of the more important emerging areas of behavioral research in auditing, belief updating, is the focus of Stephen Asare and William Messier, Jr. in their article, "A Review of Audit Research Using the Belief-Adjustment Model." The first part of the article provides a review of the model with comments on encoding, processing, adjustment and model predictions. In the second part of the article, the authors present findings from Hogarth and Einhorn's 1990 study and then from several other recent audit-related studies. In the final portion of the article, the authors provide insight into areas for potential research.

The fifth article, "Using Experimental Economics in Auditing Research," investigates how research developed in the disciplines of economics and psychology is applied in accounting and auditing. While relating relevant research, Ronald King, the author, develops the models of accounting and auditing as economic institutions and then looks at the ramifications of such models on a topical basis. The article is concluded with a presentation of issues which could be the subject of future research.

The results of an experimental study of auditors' going-concern judgments is presented in "Predictive Bankruptcy Judgments by Auditors: A Probabilistic Approach." This most timely article begins with a review of relevant research and the audit judgment model. The authors, William Dilla, Richard File, Ira Solomon and Lawrence Tomassini, conclude that the probabilistic judgment framework which they develop may provide significant empirical and theoretical differences from the traditional bankruptcy evaluations.

The final chapter, "A Test of the Relationship Between Task Structure and Decision Aids Type in Auditing," by Mohammad Abdolmohammadi, is a study of the decision process, task structure and decision aids. The author employs the Simon model to investigate the relationship between task structure and perceived applicable decision aids.

As you read the articles in this volume, we would like you to be aware of those who helped us bring it to you. We express our appreciation to Sandra Kirkby for help in managing the project; George Radford for assisting with the figures; David Brinberg, the series editor for Springer-Verlag, for his assistance throughout the project; and the staff at Springer-Verlag for their patience, skills, and their ready answers to the innumerable questions. Finally, we thank the group of authors for their contributions, which really made this work possible.

We look forward to your comments and suggestions.

Lawrence A. Ponemon
Babson Park, MA

David R. L. Gabhart
Waltham, MA

Contents

1
Experimental Research and the Distinctive Features of Accounting Settings*

Robert Libby**

This chapter will examine major changes that have taken place in the experimental literature since the early 1980s and will use this as a point of departure to discuss future directions. Specifically, it will concentrate on two categories of research that have taken directions different from the earlier work discussed in Nick Dopuch's (1990) review: studies of the effects of knowledge and examinations of the impact of incentives and markets. In addition, studies of the effects of other environmental attributes of accounting settings will be discussed briefly. This chapter also limits its scope to those topics normally considered to be part of human information processing or behavioral decision theory research and work in experimental economics, which directly relates to human information processing issues. This results in the exclusion of a great deal of important research.

Behavioral Decision Theory Research in the Early 1980s

By the early 1980s, accounting research based on behavioral decision theory was well established in the major accounting journals, accounting

---

*This paper was presented at the University of Illinois Golden Jubilee Symposium, June 1990, and is reprinted from *The State of Accounting as We Enter the 1990's* with permission of the author and the University of Illinois.

**The author would like to thank Vic Bernard, Rob Bloomfield, Jon Davis, Nick Dopuch, Marlys Lipe, Joan Luft, Ira Solomon, and Dick Thaler for their helpful comments.

for perhaps more activity than any other area except for capital markets research. Libby and Lewis (1982) cited 61 articles and working papers in the area produced in the five years since our initial 1977 review. This represented more than a two-fold increase in activity over the prior six years. By this time, two monographs, my own (Libby, 1981) and Bob Ashton's (1982), also had been published. These provided a needed bridge to the literature for interested students and future researchers.

Both books provide similar descriptions of the goals and general approach taken in this research. Behavioral decision-making research in accounting focuses on individual and small-group decision making in accounting contexts. Most of the research conducted in this area is aimed at evaluating current decision-making performance and understanding its underlying determinants. These are seen as necessary conditions for meeting the ultimate goal of improving decision making. This emphasis on describing and understanding important accounting phenomena is similar to the emphasis in capital markets research discussed by Vic Bernard (1990).

Behavioral decision-making research provides both direct and indirect benefits. As Dopuch (1990) suggested, understanding the determinants of decision performance furnishes a basis to develop training programs and decision aids that take advantage of human decision-making strengths and offset specific human weaknesses. Perhaps more importantly, it provides a better basis to explain the existence of attributes of accounting institutions and practices to our students and a more complete framework for future research.

Following the basic psychology literature, the great majority of earlier studies focused on the impact of decision makers' basic cognitive abilities and deficiencies on decision performance. Most of this research was conducted within two paradigms, which focus on the ability to combine multiple cues into an overall judgment or choice, that is, the lens model (see, e.g., Libby, 1975; Joyce, 1976) and probability judgment paradigms (see e.g., Joyce & Biddle, 1981b; Beck, Solomon, & Tomassini, 1985). These paradigms were useful, because of both their emphasis on decision performance in an uncertain environment and their ability to partition the effects of different factors such as consistency and cue usage on performance.

The characteristics of accounting judgments have been found to be similar in many respects to those of other professionals. Information processing limitations such as limited short-term memory, selective attention, lack of cognitive control, and others (which one might say determine the costs of thinking) appear to result in systematic and persistent decision errors in some important accounting situations. Clearly, there are a number of important cognitive tasks that humans are not well-wired to solve. I agree with Dopuch (1990) that many of these findings are important and have had a major impact on accounting thought and practice. However, as he suggests, much of the research in the early 1980s had become repetitive and methodologically bound. The lens model and probabilistic judgment paradigms continue to be very useful, particularly because of their performance emphasis. However, lack of innovation in their application and exclusive reliance on related methodologies unnecessarily restricted the focus of research. The major failing of this earlier research was that it did not capture much of the richness of accounting decision settings.

New Directions in the Mid-1980s

In the mid-1980s, much of behavioral decision-making research in accounting dramatically changed direction and began to explore the effects of attributes of accounting decision settings that distinguish them from those commonly examined by psychologists. Principal among these are two sets of factors: the wealth of task-related knowledge that experienced accountants and users bring to their tasks and the existence of high stakes and different types of market structures in many accounting settings. Other environmental attributes such as the existence of unusual hierarchical group settings, time pressure, decision structuring aids, and others also have received attention. Examining these issues has required innovative use of existing paradigms and experimentation with new paradigms.

A complete understanding of the determinants of accounting decision performance requires that the impact of these more distinctive characteristics of accounting settings also be examined. As I will suggest later, it also may be part of accountants' comparative advantage to investigate these issues. The emphasis on these distinctive features of accounting judgments has not only expanded our own understanding of these phenomena, but has also brought much of experimental research in accounting to the forefront of developments in cognitive and social psychology and economics. In the remainder of the chapter, I will focus on recent research that has examined the two sets of issues just described. Research examining additional distinctive attributes of accounting settings also will be discussed briefly.

The Role of Knowledge

In practice, more experienced decision makers are often paid more and are assigned to what appear to be more demanding tasks (e.g., reviewing the work of others). However, attempts to demonstrate that more experienced decision makers outperform novices in cue usage studies produced inconsistent findings (Wright, 1988; Bedard, 1989). This anomaly was a principal source of recent interest in the role of knowledge in accounting decisions and resulted in a change in focus in research on experience effects. It led to more careful attention in recent studies to actual task assignment patterns to provide a first approximation of where smaller or larger experience-related performance differences should be expected. It also led to recognition that beyond documenting performance differences, understanding their causes requires specification of the nature of experience-related knowledge differences and the mechanisms through which they affect judgment. As a result of this change in focus, we are beginning to understand the source and nature of more experienced judges' comparative advantages.

Einhorn's (1976) critique of the traditional representations of accounting judgments and his description of many accounting decisions as diagnostic decisions also focused attention on the fact that most accounting decisions rely heavily on the wealth of task-related knowledge that the experienced accountant brings to his or her task. This richer description of the decision process has led to a variety of studies of the effects of retrieval of general task-related knowledge on decision making. At the same time, other researchers realized that knowledge related to a particular decision problem or episodic memory also has important implications for decision performance. Even in situations where detailed workpapers are readily available, limitations of short-term memory require that decision makers initially refer to their long-term memory about the current problem to test the implications of further evidence. Errors in retrieval of the previously encountered information may be an important source of decision error.

Given the heavy reliance on information retrieved from both semantic and episodic memory in accounting decisions, a complete picture of accounting decision processes must place substantial weight on memory issues (cf. Gibbins, 1984). This presents accounting researchers with both a problem and a nearly unique opportunity. The problem is that an examination of a new set of issues requires knowledge of different theories and methodologies from those employed in much of prior research. The opportunity arises because the researcher must know a field of expertise in order to study it. This puts some accounting researchers in a nearly unique position, having both knowledge of a substantive area of decision making and the psychology background necessary to examine the nature of knowledge. This is a situation where psychologists themselves often lack the necessary knowledge of a substantive area of decision making and accounting researchers may be in a position to make contributions to both accounting and psychology.

Experience-Related Performance and Knowledge Differences

The typical portrayal of the decision maker as facing a variety of information processing limitations has left many wondering what the experienced accountant or user does well. The more precise question that is addressed by the research discussed in this section is: What allows an experienced accountant or financial statement user to perform certain tasks more effectively than the inexperienced individual? Basic research in cognitive psychology suggests that experienced individuals' advantage lies in their larger knowledge store and, more importantly, in the manner in which they organize their knowledge. This discussion is organized around the two approaches to addressing these issues: (a) proper use of judgment and decision making paradigms to examine knowledge effects and (b) use of memory tasks to more directly address knowledge differences. It is worth noting that all research examining these issues thus far has been in the auditing domain.

As I suggested earlier, a major feature of more recent research is the recognition of the importance of the distinctive characteristics of accounting settings. A principal characteristic of the audit judgment setting is that different audit decision tasks are performed by individuals with highly differing levels of training and experience. The need for such differential assignment is mandated in the first standard of field work (AU Section 210) and observations of practice indicate some consensus in assignment patterns. Assignment patterns are of economic consequence because of the salary differentials paid to more experienced auditors. Concern for this issue has led to examinations of the nature of resulting performance differences and their underlying causes. Despite this interest, through the early 1980s, reliable experience-related performance differences, let alone their causes, had not been documented (see Wright, 1988; Bedard, 1989, for reviews).

Frederick and Libby (1986) present a series of conditions sufficient for demonstrating a knowledge effect (based in part on Fiedler, 1982): (1) developing hypotheses (in advance) about the effects of divergent structural or functional properties of knowledge on observable behavior (which requires consideration of the knowledge necessary to complete a task, when and how it will be acquired, and the process by which it will be brought to bear on the decision problem); (2) constructing an experimental task such that the implications of the knowledge-stimulus interaction will be in contrast to the implications of the stimulus alone (i.e., observable implications of using and not using knowledge are different); and (3) establishing a rivalry between differing knowledge elements by manipulating context factors (the context activates knowledge element, which interacts with the stimuli being evaluated) and/or comparing individuals with different experiences. Although these conditions seem intuitive, failure to meet them appears to account for the failure of early studies to find significant experience effects.

Judgment and Decision-Making Paradigms. Although the role of training and experience had been recognized in the literature, existing studies in the early 1980s were little more than exploratory analyses that either correlated judgmental performance statistics with years of audit experience or compared students and experienced auditors on these statistics. Knowledge was always used as an ex post explanation of any discovered performance differences. Little attempt was made to determine the knowledge necessary to perform different tasks, the stage at which such knowledge was normally acquired, or the process by which it was brought to bear on decision problems (our rule 1). Not surprisingly, the results of the early empirical tests showed little consistency.

The typical study of that era used policy capturing methodology. The theory section was usually quite general, relying on the judgment and decision making literature where experience effects were usually a secondary issue. This did not provide a sufficient basis for developing directional hypotheses. The typical task required that subjects weight binary internal control cues and record their response on an internal control strength scale. What knowledge is necessary to complete such a task and when is it acquired? Performance of the internal control task requires knowledge of the direction of the effect of each cue on overall strength, the relative importance of each cue to overall strength (separation of duties is more important), and the ability to apply a consistent rule (be sure of this and have "cognitive control"). The first two are acquired in introductory auditing, and the third is uncertain. As a result, we have little basis to expect any differences. In fact most studies only found marginal differences in self-insight and consensus and a slightly greater weighting of the separation of duties cues (see Wright, 1988).

More recent studies have focused primarily on developing a more powerful approach to search for experience effects and designs that avoid confounding of experience effects with other factors. Abdolmohammadi and Wright (1987) analyzed existing experience studies and indicated the need to specify when relevant knowledge is acquired to provide a basis for predicting knowledge effects. They suggested that less structured tasks rely more heavily on information that is retrieved from memory and are usually reserved for more experienced decision makers. In their experiment, as suggested, they found that performance differences were greater for less structured tasks. They did not attempt to consider the exact nature of the knowledge differences between the experienced auditors and novices and the exact nature of the behavior differences that should result. As a result, they could not specify why the behavior differed.

Frederick and Libby (1986) were the first to follow all three of these rules, perhaps most importantly rule 1, which requires advance specification of knowledge and the mechanism through which it will affect task performance. As a result, they were able to make specific directional predictions of experience effects.

The paper had two goals: (a) to suggest a formal approach for examining how the auditor's knowledge interacts with current audit evidence to determine judgment and (b) to use the approach to demonstrate the judgmental effects of a specific knowledge difference in an abstract setting. Rule 2 suggests that knowledge effects can best be demonstrated by establishing a rivalry between differing knowledge elements, i.e., testing conflicting predictions that result from knowledge differences. This condition can be met by manipulating context factors (context activates knowledge which interacts with stimuli being evaluated) or comparing individuals with different experiences (rule 3). An experimental design that does both requires that three factors be varied-the target stimuli, the context, and subject experience.

In our paper we suggested that predictions of the financial statement implications of internal control weaknesses are based on two knowledge types: (a) knowledge of the double-entry generating process, which results in the co-occurrence of certain pairs of account errors, and (b) knowledge of the associations of internal control weaknesses with particular account errors. We further suggested that experienced auditors have both knowledge types, but novices only the former. This knowledge difference was the basis for our conflicting predictions of behavior. The design used was sufficient for an unambiguous demonstration of effects of knowledge-conflicting predictions of effects of knowledge differences resulting from manipulations of context and observing individuals with different experiences. Our results support our hypothesis.

Bonner (1990) significantly extends the ideas in Frederick and Libby to a more substantive domain. She again suggests that most prior studies didn't consider the knowledge necessary to complete the task, when it was acquired, and how it will be brought to bear on decisions. She further points out (following Abdel-khalik & El-Sheshai, 1980) that there are differing components involved in the judgment process. This led her to suggest three possible flaws in prior work. First, in studies where *no* differences were found, both the experienced and inexperienced auditors may have had the requisite knowledge (they examined novice tasks). Second, these same studies may not have focused on the component of the judgment process where knowledge would have provided maximum benefit. Finally, studies which *have* found a significant experience related difference may have demonstrated the overall superiority of senior people as decision makers and not the effects of knowledge. In her paper, she separates out these effects by looking at cue selection (knowledge of cue relevance) and cue weighting in novice and expert tasks (internal control and analytical risk assessments, respectively). She concludes that both cue selection and weighting are affected by experience in analytical risk assessments and that prior results seem to be due in part to choice of novice tasks (e.g., control risk assessments).

Direct Assessments of Knowledge Differences. In all of the papers discussed in the prior section, knowledge differences were inferred through differences in judgments or choices. As a result, the judgment process intervenes in the inference process. Weber (1980) was the first to assess directly the result of a memory process (recall) and to consider relating that result to judgment differences. The approach taken in this important paper is well represented in the literature today.

If you were to ask a layperson to characterize the difference between an experienced decision maker and a novice, they would suggest that the experienced decision maker has more knowledge stored in memory. Recent research suggests that the key difference is the manner in which that knowledge is organized and accessed so that it can be brought to bear on decision problems. Weber (1980) found differences in the manner in which experienced computer audit specialists and inexperienced auditors organized knowledge of computer controls.

Frederick (1986) was the first to hypothesize a specific organizational difference between more and less experienced auditors' knowledge. He suggested that training exposes inexperienced and experienced auditors to a taxonomic organization of controls (where controls are related by audit objective insured), but that experience with actual systems is the primary source of learning for a schematic structure (where controls are related by the flow of transactions). Prior literature indicates that the extra temporal links between controls in the schematic structure will allow only the experienced auditors to recall more information about a system when that information is presented schematically (by flow of transactions). The hypothesis was confirmed. This suggests that part of the advantage of experienced auditors is that they can better recall the attributes of an internal control system, which results from having acquired the schematic knowledge structure.

Libby and Frederick (1990) investigated the knowledge differences that affect the ability to explain audit findings. Using an analytical review task, we found that, as auditors become more experienced, (a) their knowledge of financial statement errors becomes more complete, (b) they learn error occurrence rates, and (c) they organize their knowledge of financial statement errors along different dimensions. We suggest that these differences provide the more experienced auditors with three benefits, respectively: (a) more complete coverage of potential errors by increasing the chances that the appropriate explanation is accessible in memory, (b) efficiency in the search pattern by allowing them to examine more likely explanations first, and (c) efficiency in evidence evaluation by permitting them to consider clusters of potential errors that have similar evidence profiles.

Memory Retrieval Phenomena and Decision Strategies

Recognition that much of the information brought to bear on accounting decisions is retrieved from long-term memory also has focused significant attention on the impact of retrieval phenomena on decisions. A variety of potentially important phenomena already have been documented. They are categorized later by whether they involve retrieval of information about the general phenomenon of interest (e.g., internal control systems), which is called semantic memory, or information about a particular experience (e.g., XYZ's internal control system), which is called episodic memory.

Retrieval of Knowledge from Semantic Memory. While the human mind is recognized as capable of storing an almost infinite amount of knowledge, this knowledge must be accessed before it can be brought to bear on a decision problem. Recent literature has begun to examine the determinants of retrieval of knowledge from memory. A variety of issues have been examined.

Three related studies have examined learning and retrieval of knowledge about causes of financial statement errors. The original motivation for this work was Einhorn's (1976) recognition that in many accounting decisions, alternative hypotheses or explanations for evidence must be generated by the decision maker. In one study, Butt (1988) examined the efficiency of different modes of learning the frequency with which the causes of financial statement errors occur. She found that experiencing individual instances produces the most effective learning, and that summary frequency data were conducive to learning when it was present in the context of a sample of individual instances. These findings have potential implications for the design of junior auditors' job experiences, the use of case materials in training, and the effectiveness of archival frequency data as a decision aid. Libby (1985) found that both frequency of experience and recency of experience with different error causes affected their generation as explanations for analytical review fluctuations. Heiman (1989) found that the evaluation of these initial hypotheses was affected by the ability to generate alternative explanations for audit findings. Her findings also indicated that auditors did not naturally consider a significant range of alternatives and that their judgments of probability could be affected by provision of lists of alternatives.

Three other related studies examined aspects of the hypothesis generation and evaluation process. Anderson and Wright (1988) reported that generating an explanation for an event sequence increased its perceived probability. However, this effect was mediated by experience. Since incomplete or biased generation of explanatory hypotheses has been found to be a significant source of diagnostic error in medical decisions, this may be an important area for the development of training and decision aids. Related work by Kida (1984b) suggests how hypotheses may affect subsequent information search. Marchant (1989) examines the role of analogy in the generation of hypotheses in novel situations. It is significant that, even in this early stage of this literature, the link between memory and judgment performance differences is being made.

Moser (1989) is notable in that it is the only paper reviewed in this section that examines a nonauditing context. He examines the manner in which retrieval of positive and negative facts about a company affect the prediction of that company's future earnings. He finds significant effects of the order in which the facts are considered, finding that earlier generated facts interfere with the ability to later generate facts of opposite sign. When combined with findings of significant order effects for information that is presented to the decision maker, rather than recalled from memory (see Ashton & Ashton, 1988), the possibility for substantial misweighting of information exists.

Retrieval from Episodic Memory. Three studies have recognized that limits to the size of short-term memory also require accountants to rely on information in long-term memory that relates to the facts of the decision problem at hand, even when workpaper documentation is available. As a result, the accuracy of those decisions can be affected by errors in retrieval from episodic memory. Plumlee (1985) examined how experience in the design of a system or similar systems can affect the ability to evaluate the system. He found that internal auditors who evaluated a system that they had designed were better able to identify significant control strengths, while those that had designed similar systems were better able to detect weaknesses. This suggests that if weaknesses are the focus of such review, they should be conducted by knowledgeable individuals who were independent of the design process for that particular system.

Frederick (1986) investigated auditors' ability to recognize missing controls as a function of the manner in which the controls were documented. He found that presenting auditors with a partial list of controls over a subsystem decreased their ability to generate missing controls. This problem was alleviated to some extent if the controls were presented in the order in which they would be applied in the accounting system. His results suggest that internal control checklists that are incomplete may hinder the auditor's ability to recognize other missing controls. Likewise, when workpapers are reviewed, the presented controls may hinder recognition of missing controls.

Moeckel and Plumlee (1989) studied auditors' confidence in their improper memories for prior audit evidence. They found that auditors were highly confident in their memories when they confused their own inferences with actually observed evidence. To the degree that this confidence reflects a willingness to rely on memory rather than refer back to the workpapers, errors in judgment may result.

What Have We Learned?

Perhaps the most basic finding in the literature discussed earlier is that experience is a benefit in *some* tasks. We have begun to clear up puzzling findings from prior work. It is now recognized that more experienced individuals don't just improve their performance of all tasks. Training and experience provide a basis for acquiring specific knowledge that will influence only certain behaviors. This additional learning also will be accompanied by a decline in memory for other information, in which case performance on some tasks may deteriorate over time.

Existing papers suggest that one key component of knowledge that is acquired from real-world experience is knowledge of the workings of accounting and control systems and the manner in which they generate and detect/correct financial statement errors. This conclusion is supported by three studies of control knowledge (Weber, 1980; Plumlee, 1985; Frederick, 1986), three studies of financial statement error knowledge (Libby, 1985; Butt, 1988; Libby & Frederick, 1989), and one study of knowledge of their relationships (Frederick & Libby, 1986). It appears as though this knowledge is critical to many audit tasks including internal control evaluation and the interpretation of audit results, and much of this knowledge can be most efficiently learned in concert with experience with actual systems. Such findings may have implications for the planning of curriculum and on-the-job experience.

A number of studies strongly suggest that retrieval of decision alternatives and related evidence is determined by several factors, and these factors can have critical effects on judgment. Some of these relate to the manner in which the decision makers internally represent knowledge, and others relate to the manner in which information is presented to them. A number of these factors can be affected by training, workpaper design, and the development of simple decision aids. Memory is imperfect in determinable ways. As a result, these findings can be as relevant to practice as prior research on other cognitive limits.

From a methodological perspective, it is clear that adequate investigation of knowledge and memory issues requires the use of new experimental paradigms and of more complex experimental designs. The studies cited earlier have used frequency learning, episodic recall, semantic recall, and recognition tests, all of which were new to the literature in the 1980s. Work by Anderson (1985); Biggs, Mock, and Watkins (1988); Bouwman, Frishkoff, and Frishkoff (1987) and others using verbal protocols also provide useful insights in this area. Research on information search (e.g., Abdel-khalik & El-Sheshai, 1980; Biggs, 1984; Lewis, Patton, & Green, 1988; Shields, 1984) also is closely related.

Designs such as those used in Frederick and Libby (1986) and Bonner (1990), which rely on directional predictions of interactions, provide the precision in results necessary to partial out different effects. Perhaps more importantly, effective use of these designs required much greater reliance on cognitive theory *and* our knowledge of accounting institutions than in prior research to provide a basis for the directional predictions. All of these changes are positive signs of maturation in the field.

Questions for Future Research

Studies of knowledge and memory effects are recent additions to the experimental literature in accounting/auditing. As a result, we are just beginning to understand their role in accounting decisions, and a variety of questions remain unanswered. The key knowledge differences that determine superior decision performance or true expertise have yet to be uncovered. Doing so requires the joint examination of knowledge differences and judgment performance differences. As discovered in earlier literature, attempts to measure performance are fraught with many difficulties. The additional requirement that they be tied to measures of specific knowledge differences adds a second layer of difficulty to the problem. Heiman (1989) and Moser (1989) are good examples of papers that tie memory and judgment together, but the tie to decision performance has yet to be made. The reward for uncovering these key differences could be more effective training and decision aids and guidance for improving the allocations of experienced (highly paid) personnel.

In addition, understanding differential performance or expertise requires addressing three questions: (a) what do people on average learn from training and experience and how is performance affected, (b) what particular aspects of training and experience lead to differential learning and performance, and (c) why do different individuals with the same experience learn and perform differently? The research described earlier addresses only the first, the effect of general experience. The importance of ability differences and different types of training and experience in the assignment of individuals to more and less demanding tasks has yet to be determined.

Although I believe that differential assignment patterns of more and less experienced individuals to tasks is prima facie evidence of performance differences, it has yet to be determined whether the effects are of first or second order. For example, in auditing, the availability of extensive training and decision aids may attenuate the effect of experience. Likewise, audit technology and the structure of the audit team may control for the effects of retrieval failures alluded to earlier. Careful analysis of the manner in which firm audit approaches are designed may provide useful insights into this question.

Although such work may be premature at this point, further research can provide the basis to investigate the usefulness of new control devices to improve retrieval of relevant knowledge from memory. Likewise, the best way to convey relevant knowledge through training, experience, and decision aids is far from clear. The answers to these questions will be complex because aids can interfere with other aspects of cognitive functioning.

Following trends in prior research, most of the research in this section was conducted in audit contexts. Other accounting contexts that rely heavily on task-specific knowledge include the design of managerial accounting systems and conducting financial statement analysis. Future research that investigates these domains could provide important contributions to our understanding. However, the lack of activity provides continuing evidence that there are many barriers to such research.

Incentive and Market Effects

There are two casual statements about experimental research that cast doubt on its validity:

1. Judgmental errors found in psychology experiments will disappear if the stakes are raised or the judges are subjected to the rigors of the market.
2. Findings of optimal pricing and resource allocation in economics experiments will disappear if the cognitive complexity of the decision problems is increased.

Unfortunately, these extreme statements are not far from the public positions taken by many scholars. While the statements are normally treated as bolstering assumptions to support a chosen paradigm or theory, they really suggest a basic question that underlies many research issues in accounting: In what manner do cognitive factors, incentives, and market forces determine decision performance? Only recently has this critical question been subjected to serious empirical inquiry. The importance of such inquiry is made evident by the fact that three principal characteristics of many accounting settings are the existence of high stakes, some form of market, and human decision makers, who have determinable limitations and abilities. Neglect of any of these factors and their interactions leads to a sterile view of accounting decision making.

Behavioral Experiments and Economics

Persistent findings of judgmental error in laboratory research have attracted a great deal of attention among researchers in a variety of disciplines in business administration. This research, most of which has been conducted by scholars trained in the traditions of experimental psychology, also has created a good deal of consternation and skepticism among researchers trained in various areas of economics. The consternation results from the fact that the findings obtained raise serious questions about the validity of many assumptions underlying economic models. Much of the skepticism relates to the generality of results and arises from the purported lack of incentives faced by subjects in the experiments and the failure to consider opportunities to learn and the aggregation process that exist in markets. However, these suppositions have thus far been subjected to little theoretical and empirical analysis.

Only recently have researchers begun to examine the impact of incentives and market forces on judgment behavior. This research has sought to determine whether changes in the incentives faced by subjects (e.g., Grether & Plott, 1979; Eger & Dickhaut, 1982) and/or the imposition of a market setting (e.g., Duh & Sunder, 1986) mitigates judgmental error. The findings suggest that sometimes error decreases (but is rarely eliminated; see e.g., Knetsch & Sinden, 1987), and at other times it increases. However, little progress has been made to determine where and in what manner changes in incentives or the imposition of a market setting affects cognitive processes.

Financial Incentives. Many critics of behavioral research are concerned that the magnitude of the rewards in behavioral experiments is not sufficient to generate the effort necessary to perform the experimental tasks. As Tversky and Kahneman (1986, p. 274) point out, incentives do not operate by magic. To be effective, they must result in increases in the cognitive effort expended and operate through specific cognitive mechanisms such as the focusing of attention or the prolonging of deliberation. Thus, error correction will occur only if increases in effort result and the mechanism involved in the corrective action is sensitive to the increased effort.

Even if we assume a simplistic relationship between extrinsic incentives and cognitive effort, the effects of increasing incentives are far from clear. Performance of judgment and decision tasks involve a variety of cognitive processes including learning, recognition, recall, information combination, and so on. These processes will be differentially sensitive to effort. The effects of increases in incentives will depend on which process is involved. If an error results from faulty prior learning of a decision rule and there is no opportunity to learn a new rule, the incentives will have no effect. Likewise, if an error is due to a specific cognitive limitation that has a physiological basis, again, we would expect the incentive increase to have no effect (i.e., when the stakes go up, we try harder, but we don't get any smarter). However, if an error results from the use of less time-consuming decision rules, we might expect incentives to improve performance.

While applying this type of analysis to particular decision problems will be complex, I believe that it is a necessary precursor to effective investigation of these issues. I am aware of only two accounting papers to date that have investigated the effects of differing incentives on judgment processes that have been the focus of attention in the behavioral decision-making literature. In an innovative paper, Eger and Dickhaut (1982) examined the effects of using an "incentive compatible" betting system versus direct odds estimation to elicit probability assessments. They suggest that judgments made using the betting technique will be closer to normative judgments. The authors conclude in a number of places in the paper that their hypothesis is supported (e.g., p. 712). However, they indicate on the final page that, while there was less systematic bias in the judgments inferred from bets, these inferred judgments actually varied more from the normative solution than the direct odds estimates due to an increase in random variation. Thus, the results hardly suggest that the proposed incentive scheme improved judgment. A closer look at the betting procedure suggests that it was significantly more complex than the odds procedure, which probably led to the result.

The second paper, by Awasthi and Pratt (1988), tested for the effects of adding a performance-contingent payment on conjunction, sample size, and sunk cost problems. While the incentives did increase the time spent on the problems, only a marginal performance improvement occurred for one of the three problems (the sample size problem). The authors also provide an interesting discussion of the interaction of the effects of ability and knowledge with the impact of incentives.

These results, combined with those of Grether and Plott (1979) and others, support the proposition that incentives do not make the effects of cognitive limits disappear as if by magic, although they may be reduced. However, they do not provide us with a sufficient basis for understanding when and through what mechanisms incentives will affect judgment. More basic theoretical and empirical analysis as described earlier is necessary. Research by Chow (1983), Waller and Chow (1985), and Chow, Cooper, and Waller (1988) on the effects of compensation schemes in managerial accounting also are relevant to these issues.

Market Effects. It also is often suggested that experimental results will differ from actual resource allocation decisions because of the opportunities to learn from reliable and immediate outcome feedback and the effects of the disciplining and aggregating forces provided by markets. Again, as Tversky and Kahneman (1986) suggest, these forces do not operate by magic. Learning only takes place under certain conditions. These conditions are often not met in auditing or management settings where outcomes are usually delayed and not easily attributable to causes, feedback is not perfectly reliable, and it is often not available for alternatives not selected (cf. Davis & Solomon, 1989). Learning is extremely difficult under these conditions. Research by Waller and Felix (1984b, 1987) is relevant to this argument. Likewise, the disciplining and aggregating forces of the market work through specific mechanisms such as differential trading, bankruptcy for irrational traders, etc. The manner and degree to which these mechanisms will mitigate the effect of individual errors in the particular types of markets in which accountants operate is not well specified.

Empirical research on the impact of individual biases on market prices is in its infancy. As Dopuch noted, Smith (1989) has already decided that the effects of cognitive limits will disappear in market settings. Interestingly, Smith's review neglects the three studies that have directly addressed the effects of biases in probability judgments on market prices (Duh & Sunder, 1986; Camerer, 1987; Camerer, Lowenstein & Weber, (1989), all of which conclude that the effects of individual biases are reduced, but not eliminated. Remaining bias in prices is still significant.

Both Duh and Sunder (1986) and Camerer (1987) examine whether double oral auction markets price at Bayesian expected value or based on various interpretations of the representativeness heuristic. In a manner similar to early behavioral decision-making research (see Edwards, 1968), states and evidence are represented by bingo cages and bingo balls. Evidence is presented and then trading is allowed. Probabilities are then inferred from the prices. As suggested earlier, the results of both studies indicate that only a fraction of the bias is eliminated. Further, in some cases in Camerer, the probabilities inferred from the prices were even more biased than individual judgments provided based on a quadratic scoring rule.

Camerer (1987) lists a variety of mechanisms through which markets could discipline nonnormative decision makers (e.g., financial incentives increasing effort, random mistakes canceling out, rational decision makers trading more, learning from the trades of others, bankruptcy for irrational traders, etc.). The work by Camerer et al. (1989) is particularly interesting in that it attempts to assess the degree to which two specific mechanisms, learning and differential trading, may explain differences between the individual and aggregate data. They develop a design that simultaneously assesses individual judgments and market prices at different points in the market period to discriminate among these explanations. It also employs a much richer earnings forecast context in place of the bingo cage paradigm described earlier.[1] This study examined the effects of knowledge of outcomes on estimates of others' opinions formed without such knowledge (the "curse of knowledge"). Their results suggest that reductions in bias that do occur result from individual learning from market transactions and greater activity in early periods by more accurate traders. Although additional work will be necessary to clarify the results, it is clear that consideration of the mechanisms through which such differences occur will be necessary before we can begin to understand aggregation phenomena.

It is ironic that during the same period where the efficiency of capital markets is being questioned (see the review by Bernard, 1990), markets that meet fewer of the assumptions of pure competition are being assumed by many to be efficient. Except under highly restrictive conditions, many markets do not achieve rational equilibria (Thaler, 1986). Given the characteristics of the market for audit services, for example, the effects of the market on less effective decision makers and the speed of any adjustment is an open question. Recent research is just beginning to address these issues (e.g., Davis, 1989).

Those who study aggregation phenomena must be cognizant of three principal points. First, while it is true that highly efficient markets can protect less effective decision makers from themselves (Thaler, 1987), it cannot correct physiologically based tendencies in human information processing. These hard-wired tendencies will in part shape the economic environment and thus be reflected in the manner in which we organize decision making in accounting contexts. As a result, understanding human information processing will be a necessary condition for understanding accounting decisions. Second, the corrective powers of markets work through particular mechanisms (cf. Camerer et al., 1989). Understanding aggregation phenomena requires analysis of the effects of individual mechanisms in particular situations. Finally, given the characteristics of many markets, "there are many opportunities for bad decision making to have an impact" (Thaler, 1987, p. 123). Many accounting markets are likely members of this group.

Economics Experiments and Behavioral Science

Experimental markets methodology was introduced to accounting by DeJong, Forsythe, and Uecker (1985a). The most critical problem with economics experiments is the sterility of their theories as they relate to human behavior at the individual level. The model of rational economic man precludes consideration of virtually all human information processing phenomena. As a result, theories based on the model normally do not provide sufficient guidance for the design and interpretation of the results of experiments where humans participate as subjects. For example, much of experimental economics has been aimed at identifying the effects of differing market structures on behavior. Equilibrium prices are observed under different experimental conditions and attributed to characteristics of the markets such as their completeness. However, when characteristics of the market are changed, the complexity and difficulty of the subject's decision problem also is changed. As a result, either the change in market characteristics or the cognitive complexity of the tasks may account for any change in behavior. This concern underlies the casual statement about such experiments made earlier. It can best be dealt with in two ways. First, when manipulating institutional structure, attempts should be made to hold constant factors such as cognitive complexity, which the behavioral literature has found to have important effects. Second, attempts to incorporate less restrictive assumptions in economic models should be supported.

There are many small changes that can be made in an experimental setting which have no economic meaning but can have dramatic effects on behavior (e.g., use of consumption objects versus induced value tokens [Knetsch, Thaler, & Kahneman, 1989]). Without a behavioral theory of the effects of these variables that may vary between the lab and the real world, it will be difficult to generalize the results of the laboratory studies. As a result, I predict that many results of economic experiments will not replicate under different operationalizations of the independent variables. Further, since the operationalizations will be indistinguishable from the perspective of economic theory, current theories will provide little basis for explaining the conflicts.

A second issue is relevant to a portion of the experimental economics literature. While the importance of motivating subjects monetarily and lack of deception are well recognized in the experimental economics literature, they are sometimes used as substitutes for the tenets of good design. Campbell and Stanley's (1963) maxims do not lose their validity because the experiments are based on economics. They present necessary conditions for the results of an experiment to be interpretable. Camerer et al. (in press) again is a good example of an experiment designed with proper concern for control.

Conclusions and Directions for the Future

Cognitive factors, incentives, and the market setting all influence performance of different accounting tasks. Further, these factors will interact in their effects on judgment. For example, the effects of incentives will depend on which cognitive process is the source of error. Likewise, the effect of different types of feedback in the marketplace will be a function of the ability of the decision maker to learn. As a result of these interactions, failure to jointly consider these factors will result in an incomplete and incorrect portrayal of decision making in accounting. The intellectual myopia represented by my two stylized statements is destructive to our field.

This discussion suggests three directions for future research: (a) examinations of the interplay between incentives and cognitive processes, (b) research on noneconomic variables that will affect economic behavior, and (c) investigations of market mechanisms that will enforce discipline in markets. First, attempts at integration of cognitive and economic theories, though extremely difficult, are important to our understanding of basic accounting phenomena (e.g., Hilton, 1980; Dickhaut & Lere, 1983; Hilton, Swieringa, & Turner, 1988). This understanding also will require joint consideration of these factors in experimental work (e.g., Baiman & Lewis, 1989). More experimental work, which follows that described earlier, but more precisely considers the mechanisms (processes) through which incentives and/or markets will affect judgment performance, is also critical (Camerer et al., 1989). Finally, increased attention needs to be paid to actual accounting and auditing practices that we observe in the field. These practices have been developed in part to deal with the manner in which humans naturally process information. It is the distinctive features of these practices that our research efforts are aimed at understanding. The work of Thaler (1980) and Hirst, Joyce, and Schadewald (1988) illustrate these possibilities. This approach should be useful in auditing as well as managerial accounting contexts.

Other Distinctive Characteristics of Accounting Settings

As I indicated in the introduction, the key attribute of more recent research is the concentration on the effects of the more distinctive characteristics of accounting settings. There has been significant recognition that many important accounting-related decisions are made by groups (e.g., Solomon, 1982; Trotman, 1983; Uecker, 1982). Even more recently, it has been acknowledged that accounting decision-making groups are different in structure from those normally examined in social psychology. As a result, attention has been focused on the hierarchical nature of the group structure, the decision maker/reviewer relationships that often exist between group members and the effects of differential source reliability of group members (see Trotman & Yetton, 1985; Trotman, 1985; Boritz, 1986; Bamber, 1983). These studies tell us much about the microorganization of group decision-making and control devices that have naturally developed to cope with sources of decision error. Such studies also contribute to the psychological literature on alternative group processes.

A variety of other environmental attributes have received initial attention in the recent literature. For example, Bamber and Snowball (1988) and Bamber, Snowball, and Tubbs (1989) have investigated the impact of the alternative structures provided to audit decision makers in the field. McDaniel (1988) has examined how structure interacts with another key attribute of the audit environment, time pressure, to affect decision performance. Brown and Solomon (1987) pointed out the role of knowledge of decision outcomes in evaluating decision performance in management. Ashton and Ashton (1988) and Messier and Tubbs (1989) began to analyze the impact of the sequential arrival of audit evidence on judgment. Hackenbrack (1989) has called attention to the effect of the multitude of nondiagnostic information that the auditor receives. Milliron (1985) and Helleloid (1987–1988) have pointed out the relevance of cognitive factors to tax decision making. Ashton and Willingham (1988), Jiambalvo and Waller (1984), Kachelmeier and Messier (1990), and Libby and Libby (1989) suggest how research on human information processing can be employed to facilitate the development of decision aids. Obviously, this list is not exhaustive. However, the variety of topics and their close association with key attributes of accounting decision settings exhibits the healthy growth and maturation of this part of the discipline.

Concluding Comments

I believe that the key to continued development of experimental research in accounting is to continue to take advantage of our knowledge of accounting institutions and decision settings to provide a basis for the selection of important research topics. The primary immediate goal of most experimental research in accounting is to increase our understanding of decision making in these settings. Though we hope that this will lead to suggestions for improvement of decisions in the future, as in other research areas, this is sufficient motivation. At the same time, we must continue to make better use of basic theories of cognition and economics to provide a basis for predicting the mechanisms through which these environmental attributes will affect behavior. The research that I have focused on here are good examples of studies that follow one or both of these strictures.

We must continue to recognize that most accounting phenomena of interest are inherently economic phenomena. Failure to consider the economic rationale for the institutions that we study will leave us with a very incomplete picture and poorly motivated research. However, we cannot forget that the participants in these phenomena are human. As a result, economic theory alone is too sterile to provide us with a basis for a complete understanding of accounting phenomena. There are no human beings as we know them in most economic theories. The theories allow for no information processing, no learning, and very simple tastes and preferences. Economic experiments must begin to incorporate human factors. The benefits of doing so are evident in early studies that question market efficiency. Important research such as that by Shiller (1984) is motivated by cognitive theory (see also Arrow, 1982). A broader perspective leads to innovation.

Finally, it is evident that important incentive, market, and cognitive factors interact in their effects on judgment. Thus, theories and designs that jointly consider their effects on behavior must be applied in future research. Our interdisciplinary orientation puts us in a unique position to investigate these interactions. This research will not only benefit accounting, but result in contributions to the basic disciplines as well.

Endnote

1. The bingo cage paradigm was virtually abandoned in judgment and decision making research in the 1970s because the results did not generalize to richer contexts.

2
Reconsidering the Definition of Structure as It Relates to Differentiation among Public Accounting Firms

Wanda A. Wallace*

Introduction

Conceptual modeling has long emphasized a potential role for the audit firm in explaining the diversity of various phenomena, from type of audit report to propensity of companies to disclose. Researchers have experimented with a Big-Eight/non-Big-Eight (presumably, now Big-Six/non-Big-Six) dichotomy and have included, on occasion, variables to control for individual firm effects. However, in recent literature, an operational definition of subgroups of firms among the then Big Eight, which were deemed similar in terms of the degree to which their audit approach is structured, has begun to be used in various empirical analyses. A structured audit method is defined as "a systematic approach to auditing characterized by a prescribed, logical sequence of procedures, decisions, and documentation steps, and by a comprehensive and integrated set of audit policies and tools designed to assist the auditor in conducting the audit" (Cushing & Loebbecke, 1986, p. 32). Encompassed in how this was operationalized were 18 elements related to overall audit process, initial audit planning, audit program design, control review and evaluation, use of audit tools—analytical procedures, computer audit tools, and statistical sampling methods—and

*The author appreciates the opportunity she had to visit the University of Manchester in England in May 1988, where discussions with John Arnold, Stuart Turley, Peter Moizer, David Gwilliam, Richard Macve, and Don Anderson (of the University of Queensland) prompted many of the ideas described herein. The feedback of participants at the 1989 Behavioral Research in Auditing Conference, held at the State University of New York at Albany, and the comments of the discussant, Arnold Wright of Northeastern University, are reflected in this revision.

documentation and review (including standard checklists). This chapter analyzes the structure construct and calls for enhancement of its measurement, via disaggregation in future research and decision making by practitioners. Moreover, a multivariate framework for considering standardization distinctively from structure is outlined for further refinement of our understanding.

Technology and Structure: Inextricably Linked

> . . . Structure and technology are confounded in the organizational structure. Technological components are organized into progressively more complex technologies through ordering and coupling; thus structure is embedded within technology regardless of whether organizations are viewed as concrete, abstract, or activity systems.
>
> This "from-the-bottom-up" view implies that technology determines structure. Yet, if a "top-down" perspective is taken, one could argue that the opposite is true: The manner in which activities are structured into a whole transformation cycle can constrain the kind of changes possible in any individual production activity. Our point is that interaction between technology and structure is endemic in organizations and that technology and structure are implicitly confounded beyond the most elemental activities, programs, individuals, and machines. (Rousseau & Cooke, 1984, p. 355)

The article drawing this conclusion provides an in-depth literature review of technology and structure, proposes a model for considering their interaction, and provides some intuitive examples of the inability to consider either technology or structure in isolation. To paraphrase, the initial purchase of a microcomputer can be termed a concrete technological change, as it involves the acquisition of a tangible machine and the specific skills required to apply such a machine to the activity at hand. However, this apparent change in only concrete technology leads to other changes. The necessity of acquiring software and integrating the computer into the workflow alters the abstract system (i.e., performance, programs, or procedures). Then the actual use of the microcomputer changes the activity system (i.e., the means of converting inputs to outputs). Each of these changing aspects of technology systems creates concurrent structure changes to order, couple, and link equipment, people, and processes. Figure 1 portrays this prominent role of technology and structure, intrinsically related, within an organization. To show the source of the confusion as to what is encompassed by the notion of structure, consider the alternative terms in use within the

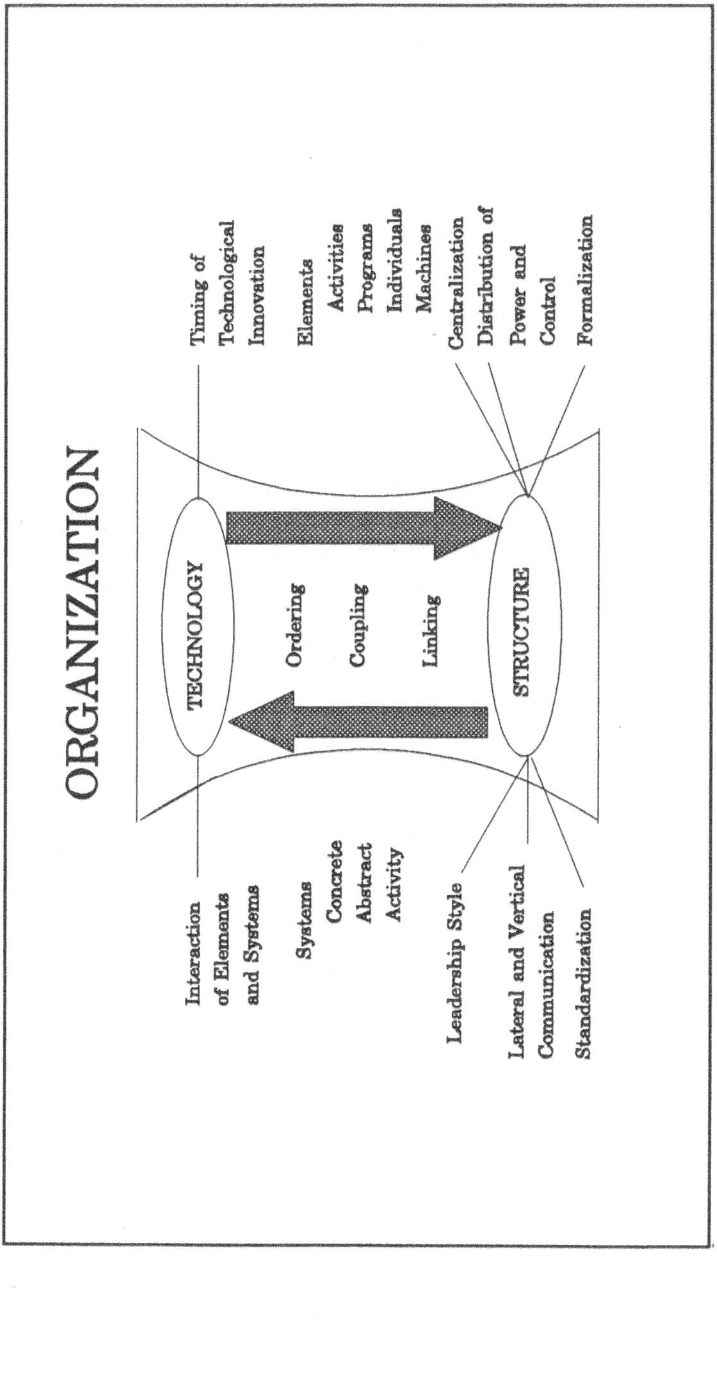

Figure 1. Reconsidering the definition of structure

auditing literature: "structured audit technology" (Kinney, 1986)[1] and "structured audit methodology" (Cushing & Loebbecke, 1986).

As conferences have discussed "judgos" versus "quantos," unstructured versus structured firms, and audit methodologies, I have found the discussions unconvincing due to first-hand experiences with a diverse set of offices and firms in public accounting. The predictable widespread application of a classification scheme that researchers can easily assign to each of the Big-Eight (now Big-Six) firms has already produced what I believe, predictably, are inconsistent results. In my view, the problem is a classic one that permeates decision-making and research paradigms: aggregation.

An Interesting International Comparison

The push toward worldwide harmonization of firms' audit approaches, methods, and documentation to facilitate the "portability" of clients' annual reports in global capital markets has been observed to be a sustained movement. Other pressures toward standardization are cited to be: (a) a more widespread notion of a conceptual framework to auditing that is based on "risk assessment"; (b) competitive pressures for efficiency and a business approach orientation to facilitate the provision of complementary products; (c) automation of audit activities; (d) technology (whereby investment decisions require general application of tools); and (e) training needs posed, in part by the faster promotion of professional staff.

Parallel Study in the United Kingdom (U.K.)

An interesting observation is that the U.K. sponsored a similar study of methodology and the degree of structure to the research performed in the United Sstates, since it was evident that a variety of auditing approaches were represented among U.K. firms. Yet, researchers in the U.K. contend that firms thought to be highly structured and quantitative were concerned as to their overmechanization and lack of flexibility, while unstructured firms were providing more overall structure and standard toolkits to be cost-effective (Gwilliam & Macve, 1988). Such trends suggest more complexity in the "structure" paradigm than currently modeled. They imply a need to consider disaggregation not merely by office but also by task. Note that domestically, wide differences exist within firms regarding how particular tasks have been structured. For example, the application of statistical sampling and materiality decision rules vary.

Importantly, structured approaches are observed in use at unstructured firms. Those firms that set standard concrete operational meanings to risk, materiality, and a mode of evidence aggregation are reported to admit that such parameters are at times arbitrary, in terms of not necessarily being right, but nonetheless being essential to standardization. This leads U.K. researchers to draw distinctions between those activities that are (a) primarily market led, i.e., due to competitive forces; and (b) those that are led by changes in the regulatory environment (nationally and internationally) leading to "common professional action." In tandem with such pressures, there will be an interaction effect created by attributes of the client base.

Creating an Image

Evidence on the likely influence of clients' attributes on the nature of the audit firm's structure is provided by the research on image- creating paths (Moizer, 1988). Specifically, research to date suggests that company management has strong views on the approach adopted by their auditors (Lothian, 1983). Impressions of past employees are considered to be a direct source of information on the audit firm's quality (Topalian, 1984) and both the attitude and appearance of the firm's employees have been stressed to be a source of identity within an organization, so that the organization could communicate effectively with a genuine and individual voice (Moizer, 1988). In the U.K., at least one major firm has used the names of its major clients in its advertising campaign (Moizer, 1988).

A Clue from Past Literature

In describing the state of the art of academic research in auditing, William R. Scott pointed out:

> What is lacking to date is an economic model that can capture the precise nature of the auditor's contribution to a production and exchange economy. Such a model should be multiperiod and incorporate rational economic behavior by all parties, including the auditor. It will show a much broader role for the audit than facilitation of contractual arrangements and will include the auditor's role in the operation of securities and managerial labor markets, as well as his impact on production decisions or managers. Also, the concept of reputation will be a major component, since this is the auditor's major asset. It is the center of the trade-off the auditor faces between short-run returns from pleasing his immediate client and long-run returns from investor confidence (1984, p. 189).

While somewhat disparaging of the limited scope of a contractual orientation to explaining the role of the audit, this analysis of our lack of understanding provides a clue to a place to start: contracts. Just as transaction economics has been applied to companies (Williamson, 1975), as a means of explaining who is on a board of directors or what types of compensation contracts are offered, such a disaggregated analysis of public accounting firms and their client base may prove fruitful in understanding the eclectic structures that have evolved in practice. Client base, for example, might entail disaggregating types of contracts that straddle classes of transactions for groups of industries.

The Role of Contracts

The mode of analysis has been introduced by two professors at the University of Queensland who contend that it is the variation in contracts that leads to diversity of auditors and their audit approach and that any public accounting firm's portfolio will be specialized according to some common contracts of the auditees. Emphasis is placed on the fact that this will not evolve into by-industry groupings (Anderson & Stokes, 1988). While the nature of contracts may vary by industry, several industries may share certain types of contracts. Moreover, within a single industry, a highly leveraged firm may involve itself in contracts that are quite distinctive from all-equity companies. If one ponders these ideas, one must agree that CPA firms will discuss their SEC versus Private Company practice, their regulated industries orientation, or their not-for-profit interests, far more than a single distinctive type of entity. If a company is in a regulated industry but is too small to be affected by such regulation, that is likely to be a more important consideration in an audit selection process than is its membership in the particular industry. Figure 2 provides examples of services offered by public accounting firms which appear to be more contract oriented than industry directed.

Actuarial and Employee Benefits Services	Government Services
Appraisal and Valuation Service	Human Resource Development Training
Bankruptcy and Insolvency Services	Investigative Auditing and Accounting Services
Business Management Services	Litigation Support
Claim Support Services	Management Information Services
Corporate Restructuring	Personal Financial Counseling
Mergers and Acquisitions	Regulatory, Investigatory, and Prosecuting Agencies
Leveraged Buyouts	Research and Development
Estate Planning	SEC Services
Executive Compensation	Tax Services
Executive Resource Services	
Financial Planning	

Figure 2. Contractual-based service classifications.

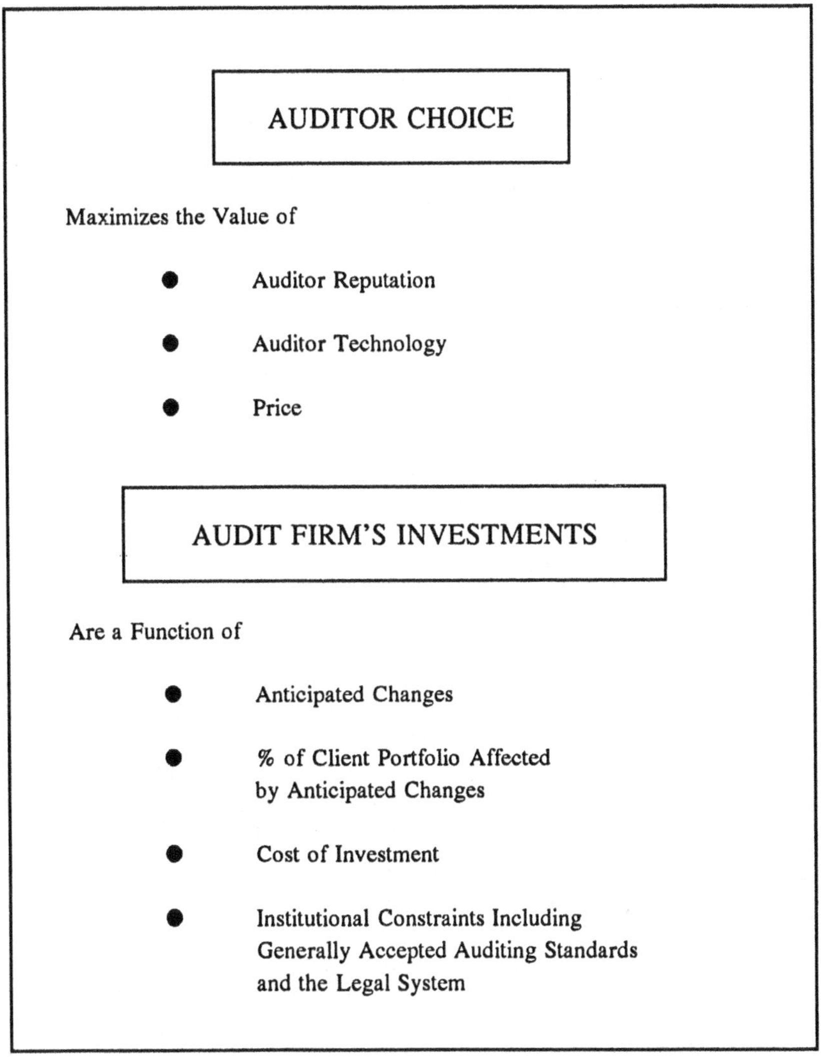

Figure 3. Demand and supply interaction.

The authors point out that auditors must anticipate auditees' contract changes and make required investments in new technology, if they are to maintain a comparative advantage. The choice of whether to invest is a function of anticipated changes, the proportion of the client portfolio affected by such changes, institutional constraints, including both generally accepted auditing standards and the threat of litigation, desired reputation, and the cost of the investment. In turn, auditor choice is a maximization of the value to the client of some combination of auditor reputation, price, and auditor technology. Figure 3 portrays the interaction of these two decision processes.

Indeed, viewing companies as a collection of contracts (Jensen & Meckling, 1976) has become the focus of finance theory. Data base management systems promote attention to transactions (Gordon & Miller, 1976),[2] and "events" theory (Sorter, 1969) in particular, when organizing information. Hence, it appears logical to view the structure of a public accounting firm in a similar manner. Given its service orientation, the derived nature of structure from the characteristics of the firm's client base has much intuitive appeal.

Some Examples

If one assumes that the structure classification of firms in the United States can be applied to their affiliates in other countries, as already assumed in the literature (Newton & Ashton, 1988), then an example of a possible explanation of differences tied to client base is available from mpirical evidence in Australia.

Mix of Services

Specifically, in comparing levels of nonaudit services, researchers have provided evidence that in Australia, Coopers & Lybrand receives a higher proportion of nonaudit fees than other Big-Eight firms, possibly achieving some product differentiation as a result. A key difference arises between Peat, Marwick, Mitchell (PMM, now Peat Marwick Main) and Coopers & Lybrand (CL) in this regard (Pound & Francis, 1981; Francis, 1984). This demarcation between PMM and CL regarding scope of services and mix of services offered would be consistent with the notion of less structure by C&L than by PMM. Since nonaudit services are expected to be more heterogeneous than auditing services, less structure may be imposed by the eclectic nature of services and the greater need for flexibility in adapting to a variety of contractual scenarios. The point is that structure at a firm level, used in past research, may be proxying for the disaggregated structure components such as nature of service, for a particular office, for specific types of contracts.

A somewhat related issue emerges from recent media coverage concerning Arthur Andersen's consulting services. It has been contended that the structure of the auditing side of operations may not effectively fit the needs of management services, and proposals are being implemented on alternative structures to affect change (Wallace, 1991). This would seem to speak to the necessity of adapting structure to the nature of the clients' contracts being evaluated or serviced in some manner, rather than trying to impose a unitary firm structure despite dynamic changes in business.

Mergers

Domestically and internationally, an interesting example that suggests structure is perhaps more geared to contracts and client base than an inherent philosophy of a public accounting firm is provided by a past merger negotiation. The proposed merger of DH&S and PW would have combined two diametrically opposed structures, according to extant literature, and yet was perceived by both parties as providing opportunities through synergy. While the merger plans and related investment were not approved at the international level (U.K., in particular), the media suggested the general support of both firms domestically (which is the context used to describe the structure classifications assigned in the literature) and in certain other international quarters (Wallace, 1986). If change of structure is tied to client base, then augmenting one firm's client base with another can produce synergy. However, if structure were an inherent attribute of the company without this logical linkage to client base, then one would predict that the merger talks would never have been initiated due to the seemingly impossible task of transforming either of the two large firms to a single philosophy.

The proposed merger can be viewed as an investment decision, along the lines as that depicted in Figure 3, which could serve as a vehicle to merge a set of structures attuned to a separate client portfolio. Presumably, certain parts of each firm's portfolio would be better serviced by the technology and structure in place based on investment decisions of each of the separate firms. Had it been plausible for the firms to expand the available technologies and alternative structures through merger, presumably a coexistence of diverse structure would prevail, rather than the dominance of one over the other.

In fact, this distinct way of looking at the structure issue may well explain some of the ineffective results of certain mergers in past years. Consider the media report that in 1977, Touche Ross merged with J. K. Lasser, combining $410 million and $40 million of revenue, respectively. By 1981, only 44 of the 130 J. K. Lasser partners joining Touche Ross remained in the firm (Brown, 1981). Similarly, a former manager of Alexander Grant (now Grant Thornton) reported that almost every problem with litigation that the firm faced arose from audits that spanned a period in which there were eighty mergers (*Forbes*, 1977). Such problems have been attributed to everything from a lack of attention to the human element (coined the "mushroom treatment" in some of the merger literature[3]) to differential quality controls. What I am contending is that perhaps they are due to a propensity of a much larger firm to place a square peg in a round hole, so to speak: the existing structure of the larger firm may not have been ready for the dynamic adaptation required to effectively service the new client base.

Research and Practice Implications

The previous observations suggest a mode for planning and evaluating mergers among professional firms in public accounting. Attention should be directed to the nature of the client base in planning the new entity's structure, rather than imposing an acquisition mentality onto the merger. Longitudinal examination of structure (firm-wide, but more importantly along the various disaggregated bases discussed herein) before and after such mergers could offer considerable insight as to the viability of the contractual-oriented view of structure that is described herein.

The Inconsistencies in the Literature to Date

Further evidence of the unsatisfactory nature of the current approach to considering structure is provided by the mounting, though still early, empirical evidence of a contradictory nature. While methodological problems may account for some of the differences noted, the focus of this paper is on the problems related to how the structure construct has been operationalized to date: on an aggregated basis. Consider the following disparate results.

Market Studies

Following expectations formed from the structure notion currently vogue in the auditing literature, Williams and Dirsmith (1987) hypothesized:

1. "Structure-oriented auditing firms complete audits on a more timely basis, irrespective of the audit difficulties they encounter, than more judgmentally oriented firms" (p. 13).
2. "Judgmentally oriented auditing firms complete audits more slowly when they involve unanticipated financial reporting problems than more structure-oriented firms" (p. 13).[4]

Yet their findings were that:

1. "For intermediate structure firms, it appears that bad news earnings are announced the fastest of the three audit technologies [i.e., structured, intermediate structured, and unstructured]" (p. 25).

2. "Judgmentally-oriented [unstructured] firms tend to delay the reporting of earnings that fall below expectations, while structured firms tend to be associated with the early release of earnings that exceed expectations . . . the difference between structured and judgmental firms appears to be most marked for clients experiencing below expected earnings . . . auditing firms that employed an intermediate form of audit technology revealed a more narrow variation in the timing of their earnings announcements irrespective of the nature of [the] client's earnings announcements" (p. 27).
3. "Unstructured firms are the slowest with respect to expected and below expected earnings announcements" (p. 25).
4. "Qualified opinions were found to be associated with surprise bad news earnings, announcement delays and unstructured audit technologies" (p. 29).

The results appear far more reconcilable to a contracting notion of structure than the currently vogue "general efficiency" argument. Allow the following assumptions to be made: (a) bad news is more likely to be tied to contractually tied problems of a client's operations and such problems are more likely to arise in new types of ventures in which a client is involved and (b) the ability to achieve and surpass expectations is greater for a stable enterprise than for one undergoing substantial change.

Merely by invoking these two seemingly plausible presumptions, one would formulate hypotheses consistent with the empirical evidence, i.e.,

1. Clients with less change prompt greater structure in CPA firms and since these clients frequently achieve or outperform expectations (in part due to greater ease in anticipating results), they will be more expedient in releasing good news announcements.
2. Clients with substantial change in operations require more unstructured CPA firms that can tailor much of their analysis to dissimilar transactions, leading to delays in reporting—the delay is driven by the underlying transaction rather than a fault with the CPA firm's structure. (Note that this interpretation is far more consistent with the delay occurring for both expected and below expected earnings, as well as the greater incidence of qualified opinions.)
3. Clients that are eclectic, undergoing considerable change at times, but also sustaining certain operations in a rather

stable environment, will prompt an intermediate structure that is more adaptable than either the structured or unstructured approach to unexpected events, such as bad news announcements.

Seemingly Contradictory Findings

Not only does a contracting orientation appear more descriptive of these empirical results, it is instrumental in explaining what, at first, appears to be a totally contradictory finding:

1. "Greater audit structure is associated with greater audit delay" (Newton & Ashton, 1988, p. 16).
2. "Our results—taken at face value—imply that structured audit approaches tend to be less efficient than intermediate/ unstructured approaches, at least to the extent that audit delay is a good proxy for audit efficiency" (p. 17).

The notion of delay in this setting ties to the auditor's report date, relative to the fiscal year-end date. In contrast, the earlier described study focused on the earnings announcement date relative to year end. It seems reasonable to assert that the report date may well relate more to auditors' planning, while the earnings announcement relates to the nature of news and, perhaps, difficulties with the audit process. The basis for this assertion is, in part, the statement made by a representative of the SEC that by far, the vast majority of the SEC annual filings arrive in Washington, D.C., on the filing date deadline. In other words, there does not appear to be any perceived value to filing early.

If a public accountant has numerous clients with similar year ends and perceives the primary constraint (other than the desire for managers to release a much earlier earnings announcement) is the regulatory deadline, you can expect that once the audit is sufficiently far along to provide the clearance of the earnings announcement, no rush would be made to totally complete the audit and dating of the auditor's report. In fact, a reasonable assertion might be that auditors would be more risk-averse in planning and choose first to complete those audits posing a greater challenge due to the nature of the client and then proceed with the final subsequent review steps and reporting details of the more stable client base. If this scenario appears plausible, then the findings described earlier are not really contradictory from a contracting vantage point. They become explicable. In such a scenario (admittedly speculative), the structure-based interpretations in past work would seem to be inappropriate.

Judgment Research

Rather than a market orientation, research has considered the individual decision maker. The results are again somewhat inconsistent with researchers' hypotheses when drawn from the current literature's description of structure. Consider the following exemplary findings (the first of which is inconsistent, with the latter being consistent with the researchers' hypotheses):

> Contrary to expectations, auditors from structured firms did not exhibit uniformly greater consensus in their judgments. However, relative to unstructured firms' auditors, the auditors from structured firms exhibited a greater propensity to increase their use of certain control and coordination mechanisms (especially consultation with peers and audit managers) as the level of task uncertainty increased. (Bamber & Snowball, 1988, p. 490)

If one considers contracting, then the hypotheses would anticipate that those in unstructured firms are more experienced in facing uncertainty and learning how to solve problems of a diverse nature. Assuming this problem solving evolves through an internship sort of process, one would expect reasonable consensus from those experienced with such an environment. Hence, the insignificant difference in consensus between structured and unstructured auditors is explicable. Evidence of this likelihood is provided in the literature, in a study that found consensus among auditors increased as the length of time that staff auditors had been associated with the same audit manager increased, rather than with the length of time associated with a state auditor's office—suggesting a different metric for experience that may have relevance to auditor consensus (Meixner & Welker, 1988). This supports a role for internship effects and the need for disaggregated analysis at an office level.

The Dilemma of Partial Standardization

The authors of the study that does not find greater consensus among structured-firm auditors do not control for such an experience effect, but they do provide an interesting insight to the factor driving their results: greater consensus between structured firms' auditors was prevented because of the considerable effect on decision aids of different inputs, such as the subtask of assessing internal control reliability (p. 503). The irony appears to be that by pushing toward standardization of how inputs relate to outputs, rather than standardization of the inputs, there may actually be less overall consensus in decision making. In other words, in a multiple decision process, all phases require structure. This is consistent with evidence on protocol studies and behavioral research, which generally finds shortcomings in individuals' ability to describe how they make a decision or the proper weighting of cues, even if they can identify each of the cues and reach a solution that matches or even surpasses that of a statistical model.

Of course, greater consensus need not relate to increased effectiveness. The questions that arise with respect to partial standardization relate to whether the increased lack of consensus leads to better auditing. The admitted "arbitrary" decisions required to facilitate standardization may not have the desired results, even in a setting consistent with structure. The added insight provided from the contracting perspective of structure is that consensus in an individual case setting would not be expected to be necessarily lesser or greater for a structured versus an unstructured firm. The amount of consensus would be most likely to tie to the experience of the subject (although evidence to date is mixed). As long as standardization has not replaced judgment, then the degree of observed consensus should be assessed for inputs alone, or any stage not performed "by remote." Definitionally, we can say that a programmed decision will be consistent across those using the programmed tool, but that would not seem to be the question of interest. The real point is: Can individuals learn to use decision support systems in a manner that enhances decision making? Enhancement and consensus are not synonymous.

The Use of Decision Aids

Concerns over the use of decision aids in a manner that may not lead to enhancement are expressed throughout the literature. In the discussion of the notion of structure, it was acknowledged that although a structured firm may gain efficiency in routine audits, the drive for standardization may mean less attention to unique problems of a client (Cushing & Loebbecke, 1986). Similarly, research has found that "managers accustomed to using statistical sampling may be insensitive to factors (e.g., source reliability) not directly incorporated into the formal sample size determination procedure. The possibility that a more structured audit methodology engenders insensitivity (Cushing & Loebbecke, 1986, p. 43) has been raised in the literature" (Bamber, 1987, p. 16).[5] However, empirical evidence has not detected such insensitivity (Bamber & Snowball, 1988).

An interesting aspect of my research on peer review is that among the specific findings occurring at least ten times in the data base was that the use of checklists and standard forms was too extensive, making the audit mechanical rather than substantive. Indeed, this finding occurred 25 times, representing about 7 percent of the public files of 361 reports examined in the SEC Practice Section files (Wallace, 1988; Wallace & Wallace, 1990).

"One Size" Does Not Fit All

Beyond these types of concern for ill effects when applying structured auditing approaches, consider the implications of a client-based approach to structure. Effectively, it would imply that public accounting firms have determined through some reasonable consensus that a particular structure fits the sorts of decisions being formulated in relation to those clients' settings. The disagreements observed at the individual level are likely to reflect the client base with which the auditor has been associated and if that differs across individuals, then the eclecticism of outputs is not only expected but may be desirable (reflecting tailored approaches to varied settings).

The notion that one structure is not "better" than another in absolute terms is well founded in the management literature. The organizational perspective implies that no single structure is best and differences in audit methodologies are expected (Bamber, 1988). This perception is similarly apparent in the finding that audit committee members view the likelihood of material errors being discovered as being similar for structured and unstructured audit firms (Knapp, 1988).

Presumably, audit committees view the firm as being likely to align its approach to the circumstances of the client portfolio. Also relevant is the evidence that while the Big Eight have been documented to have higher prices than non-Big-Eight firms in Australia, there is no evidence of systematic pricing policy differences within the dominant Big-Eight firms (Pound & Francis, 1981). Surely, if one type of structure were preferable, differential pricing would be observed in the marketplace (assuming a reasonable ability of the market to differentiate audit quality).

Research and Practice Implications

The research implication of contracting theory is that any evaluation of individual judgments must carefully control the client base effects on individuals' approaches to problems and their decisions. For example, a real estate auditor, interested in a few highly complex transactions will likely challenge the usefulness of various modeling tools that could be very effective to auditors of similar contracts, such as a set of percentage of completion contracts for a construction company of relatively homogeneous products. If standardized tools are made available for researchers' use, some comfort must be obtained that the case being used for research would be expected to be a setting relevant to the tool's application. No inference as to the propriety of particular approaches to a given firm could be drawn until the case studies were able to capture the "client portfolio effect" on approaches to performing audits and similar services. Moreover, practice units considering the adoption of various tools or different structures should take care in testing their likely applicability to the current or anticipated client base.

Disaggregation Revisited

The concept of a structure continuum at a firm level being applicable in market and behavioral research seems questionable. If one accepts the influence of subunits on overall structure, then attention needs to be directed toward disaggregated subunits. Consider the extensive literature that documents effects at the individual level, partner level, and subunit level of an organization, such as the findings that "The organizational variables that contribute to defining a subunit's structure include centralization, distribution of power and control, formalization, leadership style, lateral and vertical communication, and standardization" (Bamber & Bylinski, 1982, p. 41).[6] These dimensions have been considered in past research on the nature of the audit team's structure and the audit review process (Bamber & Bylinski, 1982).

1. The setting of time budgets is reasonably comparable among professionals, but the allocation of such time to specific audit management activities varies among individuals. These differences can be explained to some degree by firm differences (Bamber & Bylinski, 1987).
2. Research has found that "partners play an important role in helping CPAs with the professional conflicts they will inevitably face in the conduct of their professional responsibilities. While the partner actions are not all-encompassing, they do explain a significant portion of the professional conflict faced by CPAs today. In addition to this factor, the individual characteristics of the CPAs have an intervening impact on their professional conflicts" (Finn, Munter, & McCaslin, 1988, p. 22).
3. Research has addressed the question of whether a client employee's personal power (defined as the capacity to influence the attitudes and/or behavior of others) adversely affects the objectivity of less experienced auditors. Among the suggestions of the authors who find such an effect is the explicit recognition and assessment of the risk of unreliable information collected within client-auditor power relationships (Pasewark, Shockley, & Wilkerson, 1989).

4. "The need for justification was greater in unfamiliar than familiar situations" (Emby & Gibbins, 1988, p. 310); "partners sought the greatest degree of justification . . . managers . . . require the least amount" (p. 311).

The implication of such findings is that the control variables in future consideration of structure-related matters should strive to address individual, partner, office, and firm dimensions. An aggregate "client-base" measure is not being promoted, but rather a disaggregated perspective as to office portfolio, experience influence, and transaction-economics-directed classifications is being recommended.

Anticipating Controversy

In considering whether a contracting approach fits the evidence to date better than the structuring concept currently in the literature, one controversial question may arise as to why some firms along the entire continuum are observed to use similar standardization in certain areas of the audit. Is this observation consistent with the contractual orientation to analysis? It is if certain contracting aspects of organizations are homogeneous.

Pockets of Homogeneity

Evidence exists with respect to such homogeneity. One example involves research which

> identified 48 client control attributes and their perceived levels of importance in adequately describing a client's control environment, thus serving to define more clearly this audit planning concept and to facilitate its evaluation and documentation. . . . Consistent with [prior research] . . . [Blocher & Willingham, 1985], contextual variables were not frequently associated with the attributes' importance ratings (except size and management structure), thus highlighting their generalizability across a variety of clients. Audit firm, firm specialization, and auditor rank were found to be significant mediating contextual variables. (Haskins, 1987, p. 558)[7]

Further corroboration of the generalizability to which this quote refers is provided by the empirical evidence that the dimension along which unstructured and partially unstructured firms were assessed to be most structured was control review and evaluation (Cushing & Loebbecke, 1986).

Elsewhere in the literature, audit technology has been represented as complex, variable, not routine, and in some ways unmanageable (Gibbins

& Emby, 1985). This raises the specter of whether structure is plausible. Contracting theory suggests that the source of organization is that which is being audited, rather than the audit tool's nature or complexity by itself. The implication is that a better understanding of technology might be achievable by addressing structure from a contracting vantage point. This is not surprising when one considers such treatises as that which analyzed the elements of audit structure used in past comparisons of audit firms' methodologies and reported that, in light of organizational theory literature, the elements of audit structure can be mapped into nine technology elements and nine structure elements (Gibbins & Emby, 1985).

Adapting Structure to Technology to Maintain Effectiveness

The role of technological change in auditing is described in a number of places in the literature, predicting (1) difficulties in adapting audit techniques to rapid changes in technology; (2) increased availability and friendliness of information making data security controls more critical, leading to key trade-offs between data sharing and data security in the year 2000; and (3) a likelihood of artificial intelligence advancing from current decision support software (Holstrum, Mock, & West, 1987).

In considering how to grapple with such developments, particularly through structure methodology, the public accounting profession should listen to a historical perspective, offered when statistics first became prominent in business applications:

> We aim . . . at methods of inference which should be equally convincing to all rational minds, irrespective of any intentions they may have in utilizing the knowledge inferred . . . [while] in the U.S. . . . , the great importance of organized technology has . . . made it easy to confuse the process of drawing correct conclusions with those aimed at speeding production or saving money. (Fisher, 1955, pp. 70–75)

Supply and Demand

Both researchers and practitioners have considerable interest in the market for accounting and auditing services. Product differentiation has received substantial attention in the literature. Three attributes suggested to be of interest are (a) contribution to an organization's control by the audit, (b) the credibility of the audit as perceived by shareholders and creditors, and (c) the importance of product line (Simunic & Stein, 1987). Applying a contractual orientation for analysis, we would expect both (a) and (c) to be conditioned on the nature of the client base, with (b) being the result of effective performance.

Scale economies of larger firms, managers' stockholdings, and the riskiness of company cash flows are noted to be determinants of auditor choice for new issues in the marketplace, as are the form of the offering and the underwriter's reputation (Simunic & Stein, 1986). These dimensions tie to Figure 3 and the role of cash flows and size strengthens the contention that structure is influenced by client base.

Complementary Services

An interaction between the offering of complementary services and reputation from the perspective of advantages to long-term associations, is discussed in the literature (Wallace, 1987). The investments necessary by a public accounting firm to adapt its structure to its client base require a reasonable amount of client retention. As one practitioner has observed,

> The auditing firm which does the best job of balancing the three factors that must be considered when providing service to clients—management of risk, efficient conduct and reporting of the audit, and delivering values that are held in the highest regard by that client—is the auditing firm that, in the long run, will be able to differentiate itself from its competition. (Osharow, 1986, p. 104)

The Challenge

To better understand how various firms have taken up the gauntlet to compete in highly diverse ways, I propose that future inquiries proceed beyond the structure continuum in current use and try to develop a far more descriptive model. That model is projected to include primary attention to the client base at a disaggregated level,[8] as it relates to individual staff members' experiences. Market researchers can begin to explore portfolio composition at the firm level, while behaviorists need to fine-tune their measurements of experience and client bases relevant to the particular subjects being studied. Attention should be given to the dynamic versus static nature of observable structure. Moreover, tasks need to be disaggregated into structured and unstructured components of the decision process. In a prescriptive sense, public accounting firms would be well advised to analyze available structure alternatives relative to their client base and to expect requirements for incremental investments and changes to such structure as new lines of business are added or other firms are acquired. Care should be taken to limit risk exposure as it relates to premature standardization or partial standardization, with efficiency always being evaluated in tandem with effectiveness.

Endnotes

1. Note that this study classified (a) as structured firms: Deloitte Haskins & Sells; Touche Ross (now Deloitte Touche); Peat, Marwick, Mitchell (now Peat, Marwick, Main); (b) as intermediate structured firms: Arthur Young, and Ernst & Whinney (now Ernst & Young); Arthur Andersen; and (c) as judgmental firms: Coopers & Lybrand and Price Waterhouse, and then proceeded to analyze the nature of voting patterns on the Auditing Standards Board.

   It is interesting to note that despite the criticism herein of the aggregate metric for structure, the successful recent mergers have involved CPA firms within the same group, as identified by Kinney (1986). See Berton (1989, May 24 and July 7) for associated stories.

2. The need to facilitate adaptability via information systems by monitoring external market information, increasing timeliness, and highlighting problems is stressed in such literature. More decentralization and compartmentalization are recommended when more heterogeneous environments—both market and technologies—are faced operationally. Thus, a subunit focal point evolves.

3. The term is descriptive, as the idea is that you keep employees in the dark and then "can" them.

4. In fairness, these researchers expressed concern over a relationship of their dependent variable with differential clients across auditors, but the only attribute considered to test for this concern was a volatility of sales metric, which does not effectively address the contract orientation described herein.

5. Note that Bamber, Snowball, and Tubbs (1989) report that professional staff's perceptions are consistent with Cushing and Loebbecke's (1986) hypotheses. In other words, seniors in structured firms perceive their tasks as more analyzable and procedures to be more formalized.

6. This review article includes discussion of the work in the 1960s on audit firm structure, focusing on the bureaucratic nature of organizations.

7. Note that in this study, specialization was assumed to exist if 20 percent or more of the office's chargeable hours were for clients in the same industry as the referent client.

8. The relevance of client base would seem to be particularly evident in the descriptions of why the Arthur Andersen and Price Waterhouse proposed merger failed. See Sommer (1989) and Crane (1989).

3
A Model of Audit Judgment: Cognition in a Professional Context

Urton Anderson, Lisa Koonce, and Garry Marchant

Some twenty years ago the sociologist Talcott Parsons (1968) wrote of the importance of the professional in the structure of modern societies. More recently, Abbott wrote of the extensive influence of professionals in our lives: "They heal our bodies, measure our profits, save our souls" (1988, p. 1). Modern society continues to become more dependent on the judgments of professionals such as lawyers, physicians, and accountants. This increased dependence appears to be a natural consequence of both the general expansion of human knowledge and the efficiencies that arise from specialization. Professional judgments are characterized by the wealth of domain-specific knowledge that the professional brings to the judgment task and the existence of high stakes in many judgment settings. It is precisely this application of domain-specific knowledge in light of such high stakes that constitutes the essence of professional judgment.

Given the significant role of professionals in today's society, the limited amount of attention that professional judgment has received from cognitive psychologists is surprising. The attention professional judgment has received is focused primarily on how well those judgments are made (Dowie & Elstein, 1988). Just as important, though, is the issue of how those judgments are made (Jacoby, Troutman, Kuss, & Mazursky, 1984). This chapter describes the cognitive processes by which a particular group of professionals, the auditors of financial statements, use their knowledge to form professional judgments. That is, we attempt to explain how audit judgments are made. By using the cognitive theory of induction as outlined by Holland, Holyoak, Nisbett, and Thagard (1986), the chapter describes how the auditor acquires and retains domain-specific knowledge; how he or she applies such knowledge in situations requiring professional audit judgment; and how the auditor modifies such knowledge through experience and formal training. The key conceptual variable in the cognitive theory of induction is the *mental model,* which is a dynamic representation of the judgment situation or problem. The raw materials of mental models are rules that relate conditions to actions and that represent various concepts and procedures. It is argued that the mechanisms for refining existing rules, generating new rules, and making inferences within the mental model form the basic reasoning skills used in professional audit judgment.

As a whole, the extant audit judgment literature is ad hoc and exists without a unifying framework within which its findings and implications can be understood. While prior attempts to develop a cognitive model certainly deserve recognition (e.g., Waller & Felix, 1984a), such work cannot be considered complete, since one or more components of a comprehensive account of professional judgment (e.g., how knowledge is used to solve problems) typically were absent. The cognitive theory of induction, in contrast, can provide a relatively comprehensive account of professional audit judgment. For several reasons, this theory is particularly suitable for understanding audit judgment. First, through its characterization of variability, the theory explicitly recognizes the notion of uncertainty. This is important since auditors typically operate under conditions of uncertainty (i.e., where information is not perfectly diagnostic). Second, the theory explicitly incorporates the idea that problem solving is goal-directed, an important characteristic of auditing. Third, a basic premise of the cognitive theory of induction is that direct experience with a task leads to learning and, eventually, to expertise. Although learning can also be accomplished through formal instruction, or education, the cognitive theory of induction suggests that it is more efficient and effective when accomplished via direct experience. Since auditors characterized as "expert" are those who have learned or acquired a large body of audit knowledge that can be successfully used in audit problem situations, this theory is quite useful for describing expertise in the auditing domain.

Because the inductive model of audit problem solving provides a comprehensive account of the cognitive structures and processes involved in audit judgments, it provides a foundation for future empirical and theoretical work that is intended to increase our understanding of these reasoning and judgment processes. Understanding the process by which audit judgments are made is important not only for the auditor, but also for the psychologist. For the auditor, understanding how audit judgments are made aids in the control of audit judgment quality and in the development of mechanisms for improving the effectiveness and efficiency of the audit. For the psychologist, understanding how audit judgments are made provides insights into the interaction of basic cognitive processes with task demands in an extremely complex naturalistic environment where information processing is, by nature, goal-directed.

This chapter is organized as follows. The unique characteristics of professional judgment in the audit environment are initially discussed. Next, an analysis of why the audit environment is particularly well suited for studying professional judgment and a general description of key audit judgments is provided. The cognitive theory of induction that describes how audit knowledge is applied in problem-solving situations and how it is modified through experience is then presented. Extant audit research that is consistent with the inductive framework is presented throughout this discussion. Where little or no prior research exists, audit-related examples are provided to illustrate the applicability of the theory to auditing. To provide a comprehensive illustration of the theory, a more extensive audit example is furnished in the next section of the chapter. Finally, potential limitations of this framework for studying professional audit judgment and potential issues/questions for future study are identified.

Professional Judgment in the Audit Environment

Professional judgment is the goal-directed process of deciding or choosing some action with due care, objectivity,and integrity within the framework of the appropriate professional standards (Gibbins & Mason, 1988). Characteristics of such judgments include: (a) the wealth of domain-specific knowledge brought to the task by the judge (Libby, 1989), (b) the repeated performance of the judgment task in similar contexts (Gibbins, 1984), and (c) the existence of unique environmental factors (e.g., professional standards, societal expectations, market competition, time pressure, hierarchical team-performance settings) that may constrain or facilitate the professional's judgment.

The audit environment, like other professional settings, requires that the professional bring to the task a substantial amount of domain-specific knowledge. The audit professional must use many different types of specialized knowledge when conducting an audit. For example, the auditor must have knowledge of professional auditing standards to plan and execute the audit, and knowledge about business practices and legal requirements for various companies, industries, and financial markets to understand the implications of audit findings. Auditors survive in a competitive audit market (where mistakes are costly) primarily because they are able to use their knowledge in an effective and efficient manner.[1] Through formal training, repeated performance of the task, and process and outcome feedback,[2] auditors learn to effectively and efficiently perform audits.

The audit environment thus provides an ideal setting for examining the professional judgment process. Several characteristics of the audit environment allow it to have unique advantages over other professional settings for the study of issues related to the psychology of professional judgment. First, the audit profession has a formalized set of auditing standards, which ensure that auditors are engaged in specific types of judgments on a day-to-day basis. This standardization of the audit process, along with the common training and experience that auditors receive, increases the homogeneity of auditors as a group for potential study. Second, the auditing profession has adopted a risk-analysis approach to auditing. This approach, in conjunction with modern audit technology, has enabled audit practitioners to become relatively proficient at reasoning statistically and adept at quantifying their judgments. These factors are important since they significantly affect the ease with which professional judgment research is conducted. Similar risk-analysis frameworks are not characteristic of other professions (e.g., law and medicine). These factors, unique to the audit profession, facilitate research of the cognitive processes of professional judgment.

Audit Judgments

The goal of a financial-statement audit is to express an opinion on the correspondence of a set of financial statements with generally accepted accounting principles. When the auditor concludes that financial statements correspond with generally accepted accounting principles, he or she is asserting that there is a relatively low chance of material error (i.e., significant departures from fact, omissions of necessary information, or misapplication of accounting principles) in those financial statements. In forming an overall opinion, an auditor makes six basic judgments that are common to all audits since they are mandated by professional auditing standards. Although the auditor typically makes additional judgments during the course of an audit, only these six judgments will be discussed herein. Figure 1 provides an illustration of these judgments and indicates where they occur in the process of performing an audit.

Materiality. One of the initial judgments that an auditor must make during an audit pertains to materiality. Materiality concerns the magnitude of an omission or misstatement of accounting information (i.e., error) that would likely change the decision of a reasonable person relying on that information. A materiality judgment is necessary since, in conjunction with other audit judgments, it enables the auditor to determine the nature and extent of subsequent audit effort. Assessing materiality requires the auditor to anticipate who will be relying on the audited financial statements (and for what purposes) and to identify the decision models employed by those individuals.

Audit Risk. Audit risk is the probability that the auditor will fail to detect a material error in the financial statements and, thus, fail to appropriately modify the audit opinion. The audit profession's risk-analysis approach to auditing posits that audit risk is a function of three component risks: inherent risk, control risk, and detection risk. Selecting the level of audit risk is equivalent to establishing audit quality, since these two concepts are inversely related. Establishing audit risk is a straightforward judgment, as professional standards require that it be set at a relatively low level (i.e., typically less than 5%). The primary judgment problem concerning audit risk arises in balancing the relationships among the three component factors to achieve the desired level of audit risk. To solve this problem, the auditor must initially establish the desired level of audit risk. Next, as described in more detail below, assessments of inherent and control risk must be made. These latter assessments, when combined with the desired level of audit risk, determine the maximally acceptable level of the remaining risk, detection risk. Based on this maximally acceptable level of detection risk, the auditor selects various audit tests (i.e., evidence-collection procedures). If the test results are as anticipated, the desired level of audit risk should be achieved.

Inherent Risk. Inherent risk is the auditor's assessment of the propensity of material error in the financial statements before considering any client controls (i.e., policies and procedures that may prevent or detect the occurrence of errors). The notion of inherent risk formally recognizes the fact that certain types of organizations (e.g., real estate development companies) or financial statement accounts (e.g., accounts receivable) are more likely to have material omissions or misstatements. For example, banks engaged in lending money to Third World nations probably possess a greater inherent audit risk than banks not engaged in such lending behavior. Since inherent risk is a fairly nebulous concept, its assessment requires the auditor to consider a multitude of factors such as the competence and integrity of management, the uncertainty in product and labor markets, and the existence of nonroutine transactions. In assessing inherent risk, the auditor also may evaluate the client's financial position by using analytical review, which is the evaluation of financial information made by an analysis of relationships among financial and nonfinancial information. As shown in Figure 1, the auditor assesses inherent risk in the early stages of the audit.

Control Risk. After assessing inherent risk, the auditor makes a preliminary assessment of control risk. Control risk is the auditor's assessment of the risk that the client's system of internal control will fail

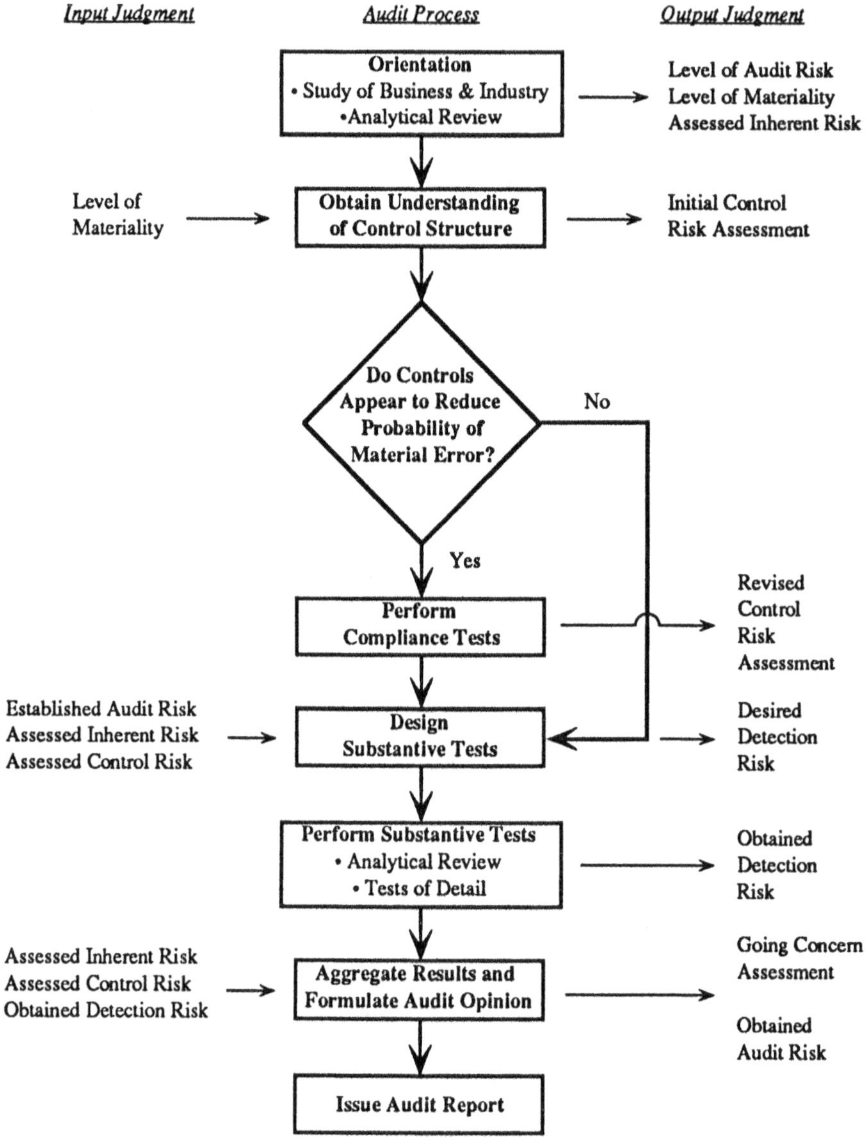

Figure 1. The audit process and basic judgments.

to detect or prevent material error. Bank reconciliations, periodic counts of inventory, and segregation of duties (e.g., the separation of purchasing from receiving and the separation of cash collection from customer records) are examples of typical policies and procedures forming an internal control system. This initial control risk assessment is based on the auditor's understanding of the client's control environment, accounting system, and policies and procedures. If the auditor believes that the client's system of controls effectively reduces the probability of material error and thus wishes to rely on such controls (to reduce the extent of audit tests subsequently performed), then evidence must be gathered through control-compliance tests to support such reliance. As shown in Figure 1, the auditor's preliminary assessment of control risk may be revised based on the results of this control testing.

Detection Risk. Based on the risk-analysis approach to auditing, once the auditor has specified overall audit risk and assessed inherent and control risks, the maximally acceptable level of detection risk is automatically established. Detection risk is the risk that errors not already prevented or detected by the client's control system also will not be detected by the auditor through two types of substantive-testing procedures: analytical review and tests of details. While analytical review is used in the assessment of inherent risk (as described earlier), it also can be used to provide substantive-testing evidence regarding the presence of material error. Tests of details also provide similar evidence and include procedures such as confirming account balances with customers, comparing shipping and sales documents and observing the existence of inventory and fixed assets. If the maximally acceptable level of detection risk is not obtained from these procedures, additional evidence is typically collected.

Going Concern. In addition to assessing the risk of material error in the financial statements, the auditor also must evaluate the client's ability to continue as a going concern for a reasonable period of time from the financial statement date. As shown in Figure 1, this assessment is made near the audit's completion and is based on evidence regarding the possibility of adverse conditions related to the client (e.g., negative cash flows, unfavorable financial ratios, labor difficulties, lawsuits, and uninsured and underinsured catastrophes). If evidence suggests the presence of going-concern problems, then the auditor must identify and evaluate the client's plans to mitigate such problems. If, after evaluating management's plans, the auditor still believes that substantial doubt exists about the client's ability to operate as a going concern, then this must be disclosed in the audit report.

Cognition in Audit Judgment

As described earlier, audit judgments involve obtaining and evaluating evidence regarding assertions about economic events. As such, audit judgments are goal-driven evidence-based tasks. A useful perspective for discussing the processes involved in such judgments is the cognitive theory of induction outlined by Holland et al. (1986). This inductive-inference theory is based on the premise that people reason by manipulating selected goals and knowledge within the framework of a mental model. Figure 2 provides an overview of this inductive process.

The cognitive theory of induction suggests that the auditor determines the goal, or desired state, for the problem situation. A goal might be as simple as attaching a name to an observed set of client controls or as complex as rendering an audit opinion on the fairness of a set of financial statements. The cognitive theory of induction further suggests that the auditor's knowledge is brought to bear on a goal-directed problem situation through the mechanism of a mental model. A mental model is a dynamic representation of the problem that changes as new information is considered and consequences of potential judgments are appraised.

The mental model integrates knowledge in various ways depending on the selected goal. For example, "going-concern problem" and "newly enacted legislation" are concepts for which the auditor would likely have separate knowledge structure representations, each containing information about their attributes. In determining whether or not an audit client will continue in existence during the coming year because of newly enacted legislation prohibiting the sale of the client's major product, these two concepts could be brought together for problem solving. Since the combined concept of "going-concern problem because of newly enacted legislation" is not likely to be one for which the auditor would have a ready-made knowledge structure, a mental model would be generated to describe this joint concept. It is through the process of manipulating this mental model that the best possible judgment eventually would be identified.

The basic building blocks of mental models are if-then rules that specify both a condition that must be met and an action that derives from satisfaction of that condition. The condition is presumably a recognizable semantically meaningful piece of information, and the action is a specified predetermined consequence that derives from the triggering of the condition. "If the auditor does not perform analytical review or tests of details, then detection risk will be high" is an example of a rule. Clusters of rules form knowledge that, in conjunction with a selected goal, enable the mental model to move toward problem solution. Such knowledge can be in the form of concepts representing general categories, such as control risk, preventive control, and materiality, or

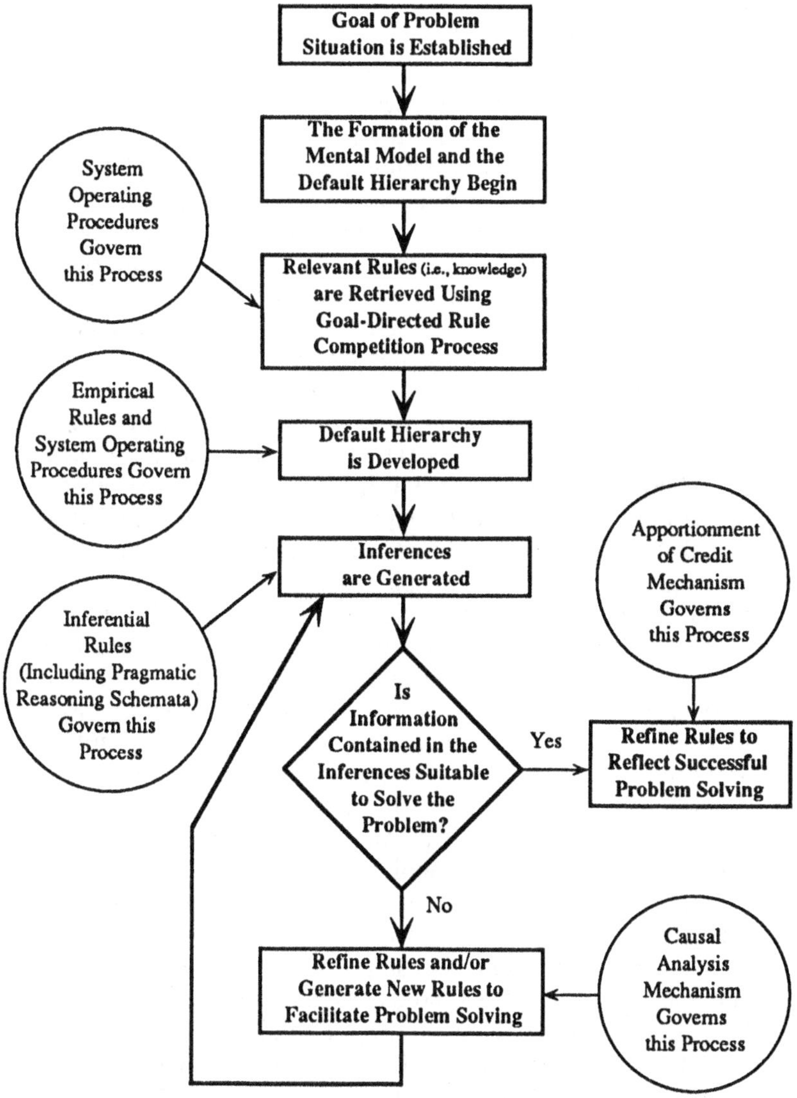

Figure 2. Schematic diagram of inductive inference process.

more specific categories and instances, such as control risk "moderate," segregation of duties, and materiality of $300,000. Such knowledge also can be in the form of procedures that are operations designed to achieve particular goals, such as assessing detection risk and testing the reliability of internal controls. Concepts are closely related to procedures. For example, the procedure of testing the reliability of internal controls is defined in part by the concepts to which it applies, such as control risk, preventive controls, and control objectives.

Context-specific memories of single experiences with concepts or procedures are represented as exception rules. Exception rules represent individual instances of concepts or procedures that are acquired primarily via direct experience, although they also can be derived via formal instruction. Default rules, in contrast, are more general rules that represent expectations about concepts and procedures. Indeed, default rules are typically produced by generalizing across a number of exceptions. Most often, such generalization occurs in response to multiple experiences with the concept or procedure. However, it also may occur in response to formal instruction or analogical reasoning. Default rules are useful since they can guide an individual's behavior in situations where he or she may have little or no prior experience. For example, assume that prior audit experience and formal audit training have caused the auditor to establish the default rule that materiality is typically set between five and ten percent of net income. Thus, when planning the audit of Alpha Corporation, the auditor uses this default rule and sets materiality at six percent of net income. Suppose that our auditor is now engaged in planning another audit, the audit of Beta Bank. Because Beta Bank has a relatively low net income (given its asset base and high transaction volume), the auditor realizes that materiality based on net income is not reasonable. The auditor decides that in this instance total assets is a better benchmark for materiality, and thus uses one percent of assets as a materiality measure. Based on this specific experience with Beta Bank, the auditor has added an exception (to the default rule) that states, "If the client is a bank with low net income, then set materiality at one percent of assets."

Evidence that mental models, or problem representations, contain both default and exception rules and that such representations are affected by audit experience is provided by several studies. Christ (1988) finds that the type of information (i.e., rules) attended to by auditors assessing inherent risk during audit planning depends on experience. Specifically, as auditors acquire additional experience, they are more likely to incorporate elaborations and abstractions in addition to the available problem information in their cognitive representations. In a similar fashion, Biggs, Mock, and Watkins (1988) find that inexperienced auditors' cognitive representations reflect attention to the surface features in the problems, while experienced auditors' representations involve a deeper processing (i.e., reasoning beyond the surface features of the available information by constructing elaborations and abstractions). While abstractions appear to be similar to default rules and the available problem information represents exception rules, elaborations could be in the form of either default or exception rules.

Manipulating mental models toward problem solution requires procedural rules that provide the basis for altering existing knowledge contained in default and exception rules. There are three types of procedural rules. The first type, empirical rules, determines how relationships between conditions and actions should be modeled. Empirical rules can model time-dependent relationships (i.e., how information currently represented in the mental model may change over time). "If the client implements controls related to segregation of duties in the accounting department, then there will be a decreased likelihood in the future of financial statement errors and irregularities" is an example of a time-dependent empirical rule. Alternatively, empirical rules can model time-independent relationships, which can be further subdivided into categorical and associative relationships. Categorical rules provide information about hierarchical category relations, such as determining category membership and assigning properties to them. For example, "separation of duties" and "rotation of duties" are included in the category of "preventive controls." Associative rules, in contrast, relate concepts that have nonhierarchical relations and merely allow one concept to remind the cognitive system of another concept by activating it in memory. For example, "loss of key customer" and "major strike" are associated with "going-concern problems."

Several auditing studies provide support for audit knowledge being structured in a categorical fashion. Weber (1980) and Frederick (1986) demonstrate how auditors categorically represent information about internal controls. Specifically, Weber finds that when auditors free-recall EDP controls from a list of computer controls (which had previously been read aloud), experienced auditors show a significantly higher degree of cue clustering than inexperienced auditors. The results suggest that experienced auditors group controls along categories such as input controls and output controls. Frederick (1986) required experienced and inexperienced auditors to free-recall controls from either a list in which controls were organized hierarchically by control objective (i.e., taxonomically) or arranged in a manner consistent with the flow of accounting transactions (i.e., schematically). When internal controls are organized schematically, experienced auditors free recall a larger quantity of their knowledge and structure it to a greater extent, thus suggesting that auditors may be more likely to organize controls schematically than taxonomically. Although inexperienced auditors do not recall more controls from one of the two possible organizations, they do structure their knowledge better schematically. In an analytical review context,

Libby (1985) notes that the financial statement errors generated by auditors (in response to an observed fluctuation) are clustered by transaction cycle as opposed to being generated in a random order. Such results suggest that auditors categorize financial statement errors in memory by transaction cycle.

The second type of procedural rule for manipulating the system is inferential rules. These rules are necessarily more abstract than empirical rules and work over a broad range of contexts. Inferential rules specify procedures that guide thinking and thus are used to make inferences, to direct the course of problem solving, and to control inductive mechanisms. For example, the use of analogy in problem solving might be controlled by the following inferential rule: "If you are at an impasse and a concept corresponding to a different problem is activated in memory, then try to draw an analogy between the activated problem and the one with which you are having trouble" (Holyoak & Nisbett, 1988). Additional discussion of inferential rules is provided later in this chapter.

The third type of procedural rule for manipulating the mental model is system operating principles. These represent innate procedures through which the cognitive system governing the mental model is manipulated. System operating principles include mechanisms for retrieving relevant rules, a bidding system for competing rules (described later), and procedures for action initiation.

While these three types of procedural rules provide the basis for manipulating the mental model, they (along with default and exception rules) must be organized into larger clusters of rules for efficient processing. These larger rule clusters provide the basis for organizing the default hierarchy, which is comprised of rule clusters arranged by their superordinate and subordinate relations. The default hierarchy is useful because it allows the mental model to make predictions in the face of incomplete information. When expectations (i.e., default rules) fail and an exception is identified, the default hierarchy is nevertheless maintained and the exception rule is accommodated by creating a more specific category. Figure 3 illustrates the relationship between the mental model and the default hierarchy.

Default hierarchies are a useful way of thinking about how individuals represent variability (i.e., how individuals make judgments in conditions of uncertainty). The initial layer of the hierarchy divides the problem situation into broad default categories that enable only highly fallible solutions to be identified. Each additional layer in the hierarchy incorporates exceptions (with their attendant properties) while preserving the broad categories as default values. The cognitive system represents variability for a given situation partially through this distribution of properties over alternative categories. Such variability is further captured by rules with varying strengths that relate properties and

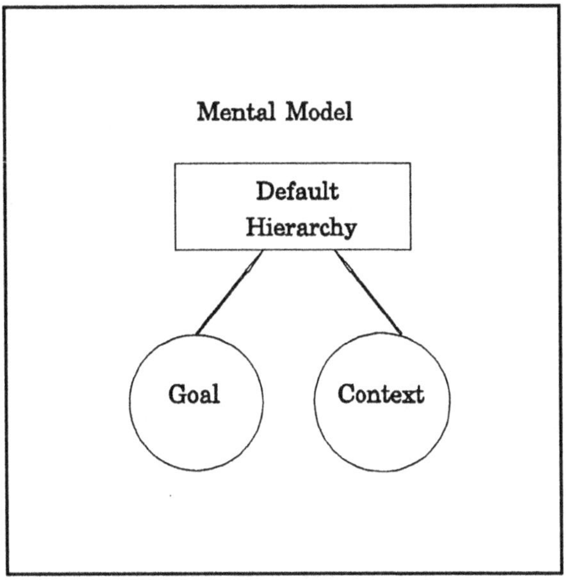

Figure 3. Relationship between mental model and default hierarchy

category membership, thus providing an implicit probability distribution. Rule strength indicates the degree to which the rule has made accurate classifications in the past and the degree to which properties (mentioned in the condition) will predict the category (specified by the action part of the rule) (Holyoak & Nisbett, 1988). The generation and refinement of rules through experience or education revise both the subordinate/superordinate relations contained within the default hierarchy and the strengths of rules. This, in turn, affects information about variability.

Auditors' construction of default hierarchies, which allows them to make predictions in the face of incomplete information, is consistent with evidence provided by Moeckel (1990) and Moeckel and Plumlee (1989). Moeckel finds that when forming representations of available problem information, experienced auditors frequently use default values rather than maintain detailed accurate mental representations of that information (i.e., exception rules). When asked to remember evidence presented in the problem, auditors' expectations about the implications of the evidence were often substituted for detailed problem information. Similarly, Moeckel and Plumlee note that auditors show as much confidence in their incomplete and inaccurate memories of previously presented problem information as they do in their accurate memories. Such results indicate that when presented with problem information, auditors generate inferences (default rules) that are subsequently confused with actually observed evidence (exception rules).

In the audit domain, Bedard and Biggs (1991) show that the default hierarchy is maintained and an exception is identified even when expectations fail. They find that auditors' acquisition and correct interpretation of critical cues as a pattern is a necessary (but not a sufficient) condition for identifying the "correct" cause during analytical review. When performing the task, some auditors were able to identify and represent the critical cues as a pattern right away. Other, less efficient auditors were initially distracted by noncritical cues. Those auditors who were able to eventually identify and represent the critical cues as a pattern did so after recognizing their inability to solve the problem (i.e., identifying the failed expectation), noting the exception, and proceeding to manipulate their existing problem representation with additional goal-relevant information (i.e., the correct cues).

Knowledge Retrieval and Rule Competition

Given a currently active goal, how do the various knowledge elements come together to form a mental model that represents the problem situation? Holland et al. propose a competition mechanism that is part of the system operating procedures to guide mental-model development. This competition mechanism differs from spreading activation (Collins & Loftus, 1975) in that activation is not automatic, but is controlled by goal-directed rules. In this competition process, rules compete against one another to determine which ones will be activated and included in the mental model. Four criteria determine the outcome of this competition: (a) match, (b) strength, (c) specificity, and (d) support.

Matching is a goodness-of-fit criterion that is a precondition for entry into the rule-competition process. A rule is matched when the conditional component of the rule matches some goal-relevant feature of the environment. Frederick and Libby (1986) demonstrate the matching concept in a control-risk context by showing how the type of information matched in an audit problem situation depends on audit experience. Specifically, they show that experienced auditors' knowledge of the relationships between internal-control weaknesses and potential financial statement errors allows them to identify (i.e., match) different potential errors in response to different types of control weaknesses. Inexperienced auditors, in contrast, are unable to identify different potential errors in response to different types of control weaknesses because they do not have this type of knowledge.

In a similar fashion, Sandlin (1987) finds that, when performing analytical review, experienced auditors' likelihood assessments for various management financial statement manipulation causes are sensitive to whether or not a company is considering going public. Inexperienced auditors, in contrast, are not sensitive to this factor. These results suggested to Sandlin that only the domain-specific knowledge of the experienced auditors was sufficiently developed to perceive (i.e., match) the importance of the "going public" information.

Libby and Trotman (1989) provide evidence that indicates that the type of rules matched in an audit problem situation depends on the auditor's perspective or goal. In their experiment, some auditors were told that they would be making judgments about the likelihood that a company would remain viable within the coming year (i.e., the going-concern assessment). Other auditors were told that they would be reviewing the going-concern judgments made by other auditors. For the auditors who were asked to make judgments, the subsequent recall of information about the problem situation was biased in the direction of their judgment. That is, more information consistent, rather than inconsistent, with their judgment was recalled. In contrast, the subsequent recall of information about the problem situation for auditors who were reviewing the judgments of other auditors was biased in the opposite direction. That is, more information inconsistent, rather than consistent, with the other auditor's judgment was recalled. Apparently, the type of information matched to goal-relevant features of the environment depended on the auditor's goal, which involved either making a judgment or reviewing the judgment of another auditor.

Since there could be a great difference in the likelihood of two competing rules that make similar matches, rule strength also is considered in the matching process. Rule strength is a measure of how well the rule has represented the environment in the past. Libby (1985) provides evidence suggesting that auditors performing analytical review do attend to rule strength when generating potential causes for an observed unusual fluctuation. Specifically, both the perception of the frequency of error occurrence and the recency of experience are noted to affect the likelihood that such errors will be retrieved from memory. These results are attributed to the relationship between the frequent or recent experience of a financial statement error and the subsequent increased strength of associations in memory that facilitates the retrieval process.

Libby and Frederick (1990) show how the strength of one rule can affect the generation of other rules. Within an analytical review context, they find that auditors who receive a typical error cause as a retrieval cue have greater difficulty in generating additional hypotheses from the same category (i.e., transaction cycle) than if they inherit an atypical cause. They explain that typical hypotheses are more strongly related to their category than are atypical hypotheses. As a consequence, the former tend to be reretrieved, which interferes with the retrieval of other category members.

Specificity captures the degree to which a rule completely describes the current problem situation. The more complete the rule as a descriptor of the problem situation, the greater its specificity. The criterion of specificity is particularly important when the default hierarchy contains a relatively large number of default rules. The preference for specific information may even lead system operating principles to override valid information at an abstract level in favor of more specific information, which may be of questionable validity. In the auditing domain, however, Kida (1984a) finds that auditors do not favor specific information over more abstract data. Specifically, when assessing the likelihood that an audit client would fail within the coming year (i.e., going concern), auditors showed no preference for specific data (i.e., data regarding the number of similar firms failing within a specific industry) over general data (i.e., data regarding the number of firms failing across all industries).

The final factor in rule competition is the level of support the rule receives from other rules. More precisely, support measures the compatibility of the rule with other rules generated in the mental model and thus is a measure of the coherence of the model. Coherence is necessary since the mental model typically operates without complete information. Moeckel (1990) notes that auditors often alter their representations of available problem information to make them coherent in light of their representations of related information. Indeed, auditors' responses to a recognition test demonstrated that their memories had been altered to induce consistency between contradictory pieces of information. Moeckel also notes that as auditors gain audit experience, this tendency increases.

Once the rule, or rule cluster, that has the highest bid is activated and incorporated into the default hierarchy, the individual generates inferences to identify a possible solution to the problem. The next section of the chapter discusses various inference mechanisms.

Inference Mechanisms

To achieve the current goal, the activated knowledge must work in concert with inferential rules to direct the course of problem solving. Inferential rules specify procedures that guide thinking and constrain new rules that may be generated. As discussed later, there are many inferential rules that can be used to generate inferences necessary for problem solving.

The unusualness heuristic is an inferential rule that links two (or more) unusual or unexpected events if these events occur contiguously either in time or space. When assessing going concern, for example, the auditor may learn that an important patent pertaining to the client's production process was unsuccessfully defended in court and that the client's major customer signed a three-year exclusive contract with a competitor. Using the unusualness heuristic, the auditor may link these two unexpected events and conclude that the loss of the patent rights led to the loss of customers.

Another inferential rule, the law of large numbers, provides for the creation of a new rule about a population based on the results of a sample of observations from that population. For example, when performing tests of details on a repeated basis, the auditor may note that the financial statement error, sales recorded in the wrong period, is responsible for four of ten cases of observed unusual fluctuations in the gross margin ratio. Consequently, the auditor would conclude that, in general, this type of error is responsible for 40 percent of all gross margin fluctuations. Libby and Frederick (1990) provide evidence supporting the usefulness of the law of large numbers. They find that as audit experience increases, perceptions of the long-run frequency of financial statement errors become more accurate.

Another inferential rule for which a great deal of supporting empirical evidence exists is the representativeness heuristic. An individual who follows this heuristic evaluates the likelihood of an event being predicted or explained by the degree to which it: (a) is similar in essential properties to its parent population and (b) reflects the salient features of the process by which it is generated (Tversky & Kahneman, 1982b). For example, when X is highly representative of Y, the probability that X originates from Y is judged to be high.

Uecker and Kinney (1977) investigated auditors' use of the representativeness heuristic in a control-compliance testing task. Specifically, auditors studied pairs of sample sizes and sample error rates and selected the member of each pair that provided better evidence that the population error rate did not exceed five percent. By varying the sample sizes and sample error rates, each pair was constructed such that one outcome provided adequate evidence at a 95 percent confidence level, while the other outcome did not. For each pair, the correct choice was the one with the larger sample error rate. Choices based on representativeness would be insensitive to sample size and thus would favor the smaller sample error rates. Uecker and Kinney found that over half of the auditors selected the smaller sample error rate and thus made judgments consistent with representativeness.

The Frederick and Libby (1986) study also demonstrates representativeness. As previously described, this study found that auditors who observe internal control weaknesses judge the likelihood of potential financial statement errors by their similarity to the most representative errors previously produced by those circumstances. Indeed, auditors' judgments are noted to be a function of the specific error stored in memory as the prototypical outcome.

Another inferential rule is the availability heuristic. Availability is used when an individual assesses the frequency of a class or the probability of an event by the ease with which prior instances or occurrences can be brought to mind (Tversky & Kahneman, 1982a). Availability is often used in causal analysis where events are attributed to particular causes because of the salience of those causes (Taylor & Fiske, 1978).

Heiman (1990) and Frederick (1986) demonstrate how auditors use availability when rendering analytical review and control risk judgments, respectively. Heiman finds that when auditors performing analytical review are exposed to alternative causes after assuming an inherited plausible cause for an observed fluctuation, their probability assessment for the inherited cause decreases. Heiman suggests that this is evidence that such alternative causes are not available to the auditors unless they are asked to self-generate or are provided with such alterna-tives. In a similar fashion, Frederick shows how control risk judgments are influenced by the availability of internal control knowledge. Using a fault-tree judgment task (cf. Mehle, Gettys, Manning, Baca, & Fisher, 1981), Frederick notes that experienced auditors who receive a partial checklist of controls as a prime recall fewer "critical" controls than experienced auditors who do not receive a checklist. Inexperienced auditors, on the other hand, recall the same number of "critical" controls in both the partial-checklist and no-checklist conditions. These results indicate that experienced auditors have difficulty generating additional controls because such controls are not available (i.e., the controls are stored in memory, but the auditors are unable to retrieve them). In contrast, inexperienced auditors have difficulty generating additional controls because of incomplete internal control knowledge (i.e., the controls are not stored in memory).

The inferential rules described earlier are relatively simple rules (i.e., simple in the sense that such rules also are possessed by other animals). People also have more complex inferential rules based on a type of knowledge structure different from that postulated by other logical reasoning theories. Such rules are referred to as pragmatic reasoning schemata and involve reasoning with knowledge structures that are at a level of abstraction between formal context-free syntactic rules and memories of specific experiences. Pragmatic reasoning schemata differ from syntactic rules in that they are defined in terms of goals (e.g., determining the cause of an event) and relationships to these goals (e.g., cause and effect). Such schemata also differ from memories of specific experiences in that they are highly abstract and apply to a wide range of content domains.

Pragmatic reasoning schemata emerge through the process of acquiring experience with a wide range of problem situations. Specifically, experience brings forth different types of problem situations involving concepts such as causation and regulation. Through the operation of various generalization mechanisms, individuals will induce increasingly abstract levels of default rules about causation and regulation (i.e., pragmatic reasoning schemata) from this experience. Since pragmatic reasoning schemata are quite general, schemata for concepts such as "forward inference" can be used for situations that may be very different from those from which the concepts were originally induced.

Kelley (1973) describes a class of pragmatic reasoning schemata, called causal schemata, that are very general (i.e., content-independent) rules that individuals have for dealing with causality. Kelley suggests that when reasoning about an effect, individuals apply the causal reasoning schemata that they believe is appropriate for that effect. For example, individuals know that certain effects may have several potential causes, some of which may be sufficient (i.e., one cause alone can produce the effect) and some of which may be necessary (i.e., the effect will not occur unless a particular cause is present). Thus, when reasoning in a forward direction (from a cause to a hypothesized effect), individuals using causal schemata will infer that the effect cannot occur if a necessary cause is absent. They will infer, however, that the effect could occur if an absent cause is merely sufficient.

Waller and Felix (1989) investigate the effect of causal schemata on auditors' analytical review judgments. Specifically, their investigation examines the association between the direction of inference (forward inference from cause to effect versus backward inference from effect to cause) and type of information about a causal relation (conditionality versus multiplicity). Consistent with Kelley's framework, auditors employ different types of causal schemata (and thus use different types of information) depending on whether a forward or backward inference is required. Specifically, when the analytical review task requires a forward inference from cause A to effect B, a forward-inference schema is activated and linked to the observation that cause A is present. In this situation, auditors' judgments are heavily influenced by information regarding the presence or absence of conditions that are required to combine with cause A to produce the effect B (i.e., conditionality information). Alternatively, when the audit task demands a backward inference from effect B to cause A, a backward-inference schema is activated and linked to the observation that effect B is present. Auditors' judgments in this situation, in contrast, are more heavily influenced by information regarding the presence or absence of cause A and the presence or absence of alternative causes (i.e., multiplicity information).

Another Waller and Felix (1987) study investigates whether auditors' causal schemata lead them to make covariation judgments that are in accord with normative, or objective, covariation patterns. The results suggest that, when performing analytical review, auditors generally use data-integration rules that are sensitive to the objective covariation level in the available data, but that they tend to overstate or understate this level. Waller and Felix also note that the ability to judge covariation is not positively related to audit experience. That is, more experienced auditors are not better at judging covariation than less experienced auditors. The latter finding is consistent with research suggesting that learning covariation patterns is difficult, even with substantial task experience (Holyoak & Nisbett, 1988).

Another type of pragmatic reasoning schemata is regulation schemata (Cheng & Holyoak, 1985). These schemata are important because they increase the effectiveness and efficiency of our thinking by describing common regularities among events. The permission schema involves rules for dealing with situations in which some action X must be taken only if some precondition Y is satisfied. That is, it captures the basic rule that "If you wish to do X, then you must first do Y." An audit example of a permission schema is: "If you wish to calculate detection risk, then you must first assess inherent, control, and audit risks." Another regulation schema, obligation, involves rules for dealing with situations in which the occurrence of some condition X requires that action Y be taken. That is, it captures the rule: "If X occurs, then you must do Y." An example of an obligation schema is: "If substantial doubt exists about the ability of the firm to continue as a going concern, then the auditor must disclose this in the audit opinion." Because individuals have experienced numerous instances of both compliance with and violations of permissions and obligations, they have schemata describing possible actions and outcomes when the conditional components of such rules obtain. The importance of these schemata is evidenced by Cheng and Holyoak (1985), who find that when individuals fail to use such schemata, judgment errors typically result.

Once inferences are made (by any one or more of these inferential rules) and a potential problem solution is generated, it is then tested for accuracy and its utility in solving the current problem via simulation. Through this simulation, the cognitive system assesses whether the problem solution is consistent with the available information and determines whether it provides predictive or diagnostic utility for the problem situation. If feedback from the cognitive system indicates that the tentative problem solution is not suitable, then some process for revising the selected rule or rule cluster or for generating new rules must be used. The refinement of an existing rule or the generation of a new rule can be achieved by a number of different mechanisms which are discussed in the next section of the chapter.

Rule Refinement and Rule Generation

The essence of the inductive process is the modification of knowledge structures with the goal of reducing uncertainty about the environment. Such modification enables an individual to efficiently and effectively develop mental models and thus to solve problems. In modifying knowledge structures, inductive mechanisms must accomplish three interrelated tasks. They must:

> (a) evaluate the system's rules as instruments for goal attainment, improving them where possible and favoring the better ones in application; (b) generate plausibly useful new rules that are capable of extracting and exploiting regularities in experience; and (c) provide associations between and clusterings among rules in order to create larger knowledge structures leading to efficient modelling of the environment. (Holland et al., 1986, p. 68)

Modification of knowledge structures occurs in response to specific problem-solving goals and involves two primary types of inductive change: the refinement of existing rules and the generation of new rules.[3] These two types of change correspond to the first two tasks listed by Holland. The third task, the generation of larger knowledge structures by clustering related rules, is accomplished by a combination of rule generation and rule refinement. Direct task experience and feedback from the environment are important components for these three types of self-initiated inductive changes. It is possible, however, to introduce new rules from external sources, such as through formal instruction.

Rule Refinement. Rule refinement essentially involves the reward of rules responsible for success in various judgment tasks and the punishment of rules responsible for failure. One mechanism for rule refinement is the apportionment of credit to rules. In this mechanism, an activated rule passes back some of its strength to the rule(s) that led to its activation. This process strengthens the support between rules that are activated more frequently, thus ensuring the survival of successful rules. Rules also can be refined by revising the strength of a rule based on process and outcome feedback.

Evidence of this credit apportionment mechanism in the audit domain is provided by Libby (1985). Recall that Libby found that more frequently occurring financial statement errors were more likely to be retrieved from memory in an analytical review task. This result was attributed to the fact that frequency of experience and strength of associations in memory are positively related and that more retrieval properties are associated with frequently experienced errors.

Similar evidence on this credit apportionment mechanism is provided by Waller and Felix (1984b). They find that auditors' self-perceived judgment ability in control risk settings is highly affected by outcome feedback. Specifically, the self-perceived judgment ability of auditors provided with feedback about the reliability of internal controls tends to be heavily influenced by the positive hit rate (i.e., situations in which favorable control-risk judgments are made and successful control-testing outcomes accrue). Such results may suggest that auditors overweight rules responsible for problem-solving success and underweight rules responsible for failure.

Another means of rule refinement is causal analysis. Causal analysis typically occurs in response to a problem-solving failure (i.e., a situation in which a problem solution generated by the mental model fails to describe the environment or provide utility for problem solving). In such cases, causal analysis will use empirical rules about causal sequences and various inferential rules to determine why the expectation failed to describe the current problem situation. In addition, the "failed" rule will be refined to accommodate the current exception. Causal analysis also can be called upon to revise the strength of rules, to modify related rules at higher levels of generality, and to generate new rules.

Rule Generation. While rule refinement is an important mechanism for learning and modifying knowledge, it is limited in the sense that only rules already in existence can be refined. Inadequacies in these rules cannot be improved upon through rule refinement. The alternative is to have mechanisms in place for generating new rules. There are several ways in which new rules can be generated.

Generalization is one such mechanism for generating new rules. There are two types of generalization: instance-based and condition-simplifying. In instance-based generalization, a new more global rule is produced by associating two or more features of existing exception rules. Such generalization is triggered by exception rules that have similar properties or conditions. In the auditing domain, for example, the auditor may possess the following two rules related to audit materiality:

1. If the client is a bank, then base materiality on total assets.
2. If the client is an insurance company, then base materiality on total assets

Using instance-based generalization, the auditor may generate the following rule: "If the client is a financial institution, then base materiality on total assets."

In condition-simplifying generalization, an existing rule is made more general by dropping or ignoring part of its condition or by grading the intersection of two or more rules. For example, when assessing inherent risk, the auditor may have the following rule: "If the client is a savings and loan and is located in Texas, then inherent risk is high." This rule can be made more general by dropping the condition stating the client must be located in Texas, producing the rule: "If the client is a savings and loan, then inherent risk is high."

If the generalization is successful (i.e., it assists in problem solving), it will survive and gain strength and the original rules will no longer serve as exceptions. However, if the generalization is not successful, it may be removed from the default hierarchy or, alternatively, it may be included in the default hierarchy (with the original rules) in a form resembling something between a generalization and an exception.

Although generalization is useful because it facilitates knowledge refinement, generalized rules may subsequently produce erroneous judgments. Consequently, the accumulated knowledge in the generalized rules can be augmented by producing exception rules. The process of specialization creates a new rule for the special case by augmenting the attributes of an existing rule or by adjusting the expectations generated by an existing rule to include an observed outcome. The more specialized rule protects the generalized rule from frequent judgment failures. For example, suppose an auditor has the following rule for situations involving the assessment of control risk: "If a clerk handles cash *and* makes accounting entries, then control risk is high." Then the auditor observes an instance in which this lack of segregation of duties does not result in errors or irregularities. The auditor further notes that in this instance a supervisor closely monitored the clerk's work. Consequently, the auditor develops the new more-specialized rule: "If a clerk handles cash and makes accounting entries and is *not* closely supervised, then control risk is high."

Analogy is another mechanism for generating new rules. Analogy is probably the most complex mechanism for rule generation, since it involves both generalization and specialization. Analogy is used to generate new rules applicable to problem solution by transferring knowledge from a familiar domain to an unfamiliar domain. Indeed, the usefulness of analogy depends upon the individual's ability to recognize the "significant similarity" in problem representations between familiar and unfamiliar domains.

Marchant (1989) shows how auditors performing analytical review use analogical reasoning to generate potential causes. Specifically, both experienced and inexperienced auditors are noted to use analogical reasoning in a similar fashion when generating potential causes for an unfamiliar situation. However, for a more familiar situation, strategies based on domain-specific knowledge are used and a difference in performance between the experienced and inexperienced auditors becomes more apparent.

Abduction is the generation of a rule to solve a problem that requires an explanation. For example, assume that the auditor observes that her audit client, who has engaged in a number of nonroutine transactions, has several material errors in the financial statements. The auditor may form the general rule that clients who engage in nonroutine transactions tend to experience material financial statement errors, because that rule would provide an explanation for the observed errors. In this situation, the new rule does not summarize knowledge about a number of instances, but it produces a generalization from one instance.[4] To ensure that an explanatory hypothesis generated by abduction is right, individuals can employ the mechanism of multiple abduction, which involves showing that the rule explains a variety of facts.

Bedard and Biggs (1991) demonstrate that auditors who make problem-solving errors when performing analytical review do not tend to engage in multiple abduction. That is, auditors making problem-solving errors typically reason with one or two cues at a time instead of attempting to reason with the combination of all critical cues. Since the basis for recognizing all of the cues as a pattern is knowledge of accounting and auditing principles, Bedard and Biggs suggest that these auditors do not have or are unable to access (match) such knowledge structures while performing the task.

Rule coupling is another mechanism for generating new rules. Rule coupling creates associations between rules and is triggered when unassociated rules are active in the same context or close in temporal order. The rationale for this kind of triggering condition is that rules active in the same context are often mutually relevant, and rules active in close temporal order frequently reflect causal relations. Rules generated by rule coupling will survive and gain in strength only if they are useful to the cognitive system, as with other types of generated rules.

In the auditing domain, Koonce (1990) provides evidence suggesting that the degree to which rule coupling occurs in a given situation depends on whether a causal explanation has been constructed. Within an analytical review setting, she finds that experienced auditors asked to generate an explanation for a hypothesized cause engage in a greater amount of causal reasoning, or rule coupling, than do auditors who are not asked to provide a written explanation. Such results suggest that auditors do not store previously generated scenarios, or rule clusters, for potential causes of unusual fluctuations. Rather, such rule clusters are generated at the time of explanation.

In contrast, Anderson and Wright's (1988) study of auditors' control risk judgments indicates that experienced auditors store previously generated scenarios, or rule clusters, in memory for various hypothetical payroll system events. Such previously generated rule clusters are recalled from memory (and included in the mental model) both by auditors asked to provide a written explanation and those not asked to do so. Consequently, judgments about the likelihood of the payroll events do not depend on whether a written explanation has been developed.

A final source of the generation of new rules is education. Rules acquired through education are similar to rules acquired by induction. That is, they will compete with the rest of the rules in the cognitive system's possession for the right to represent the problem situation. However, they also can act very differently from rules acquired by induction. Evidence has shown that rules acquired through education often will not be beneficial if the individual is unable to encode observed events so as to link them to those rules (Cheng, Holyoak, Nisbett, & Oliver, 1986).

In the audit domain, Butt (1988) shows that the manner in which error frequency knowledge is acquired by auditors affects their subsequent frequency judgments. Specifically, her results indicate that frequency judgments based on direct experience (i.e., individual presentations of financial statement errors) are more accurate than those based on indirect experience (i.e., presentation of summary data). Since knowledge acquired by direct experience is similar to rules acquired by induction, and knowledge acquired by indirect experience is similar to acquiring rules by education, Butt's study highlights the importance of learning by induction, or direct experience.

Summary and Auditing Example

As described in the previous sections of this chapter, induction theory is based on the premise that people reason by manipulating selected goals and knowledge within the framework of a mental model. Knowledge is acquired through direct experience or education and is used in response to goal-directed problem situations. A goal-directed rule competition process (where rule matching, strength, specificity, and support are the screening criteria) determines which rules will be activated and included in the default hierarchy. The default hierarchy comprises clusters of default, exception, and procedural rules which are organized based on their superordinate and subordinate relations. The default hierarchy is useful because it allows the mental model to make predictions in the face of incomplete information. Once the default hierarchy is established, inferential rules are used as necessary to make inferences about the problem situation. This inference process is a key element in the development of potential problem solutions. If simulation indicates that the potential problem solutions are not suitable, then various rule refinement and rule generation mechanisms exist to manipulate the mental model. Once the default hierarchy is in a form suitable for problem solving and all necessary inferences have been made, the problem solver will render a judgment or decision about the problem situation. Such judgments and decisions will necessarily be made under conditions of uncertainty. That is, both the distribution of properties over alternative categories and rules with varying strengths represent variability within the environment, thus leading to judgments and decisions made under uncertainty.

As cognitive systems are engaged in making inferences and solving problems, they are constantly creating and revising rules and rule clusters (i.e., they are engaged in learning). Through these refinement and generation processes, knowledge expands from simple rules and rule clusters to larger and more efficiently organized rule clusters. These larger and more efficiently organized rule clusters may themselves be transformed and recombined so that knowledge grows in what Holyoak and Nisbett (1988) call a "bootstrapping" fashion. This acquisition and transformation of knowledge through experience in a particular domain is an important component to the development of expertise in that domain.

There are at least two implications of the development of expertise for problem solving. First, the development of larger and more efficiently organized knowledge structures enhances the development of mental models.

Specifically, such knowledge structures allow more complete problem representations, or mental models, to be developed; this, in turn, facilitates subsequent problem solving. As previously discussed, several auditing studies (Biggs et al., 1988; Christ, 1988) have shown that more experienced auditors (who presumably have larger and more efficiently organized knowledge bases) develop problem representations, or mental models, that are more complete than those developed by auditors with less experience.

Second, the development of larger and more efficiently organized knowledge structures enhances the refinement and generation of rules. A basic premise of induction is that once one rule has been formed, related rules will be easier to generate since much of the rule encoding and clustering work has already been performed. Such cognitive behavior can facilitate problem solving by causing individuals, when constrained by limited cognitive resources, to encode only that portion of the environment that is already involved in useful regularities. Such behavior is particularly important in the audit domain since some audit tasks are not repetitive in nature, thereby limiting the amount of direct experience with the task (Davis & Solomon, 1989).

To provide a comprehensive illustration of this cognitive process of induction, an audit-related example is presented. Specifically, this example describes a situation in which the auditor is performing analytical review (as part of the process of assessing inherent risk) to identify potential material error in the financial statements. This example illustrates that, in order to successfully perform the analytical review, the auditor must determine a goal for the audit problem situation, use current problem information and prior knowledge to develop a mental model, and manipulate the mental model to solve the audit problem.

Assume that the auditor is engaged in assessing inherent risk in conjunction with the audit of XYZ Corporation. As part of this task, the auditor decides to perform an analytical review to highlight areas where there may be a heightened potential for material error. Initially, the auditor gathers information about the client and its operations, including financial statement information for the current and prior years. When evaluating this information, the auditor identifies unusual increases (from the prior year) in ending inventory, cost of goods sold, and net income and notes an unusual decrease in selling, general and administrative (SG&A) expenses. Because of these unexpected fluctuations and their potential impact on audit planning, the auditor decides to investigate further. The auditor's goal is to determine the cause of these fluctuations. Figure 4 provides an illustration of this example based on a case by Bedard and Biggs (1991).

In light of this goal, the auditor collects evidence to develop a mental model or problem representation. Such evidence includes available problem information (e.g., the financial and nonfinancial information obtained from the client) and information stored in the auditor's long-term memory. Problem information is initially encoded by the auditor's perception system and forwarded to working memory where certain clusters of rules are activated and links to long-term memory are made to activate knowledge stored there. It is through the process of goal-directed competition among rules (where the four criteria of matching, strength, specificity, and support determine the outcome of the competition) that some of the many activated clusters of default and exception rules eventually become part of the mental model. Not only is the mental model made up of default and exception rules, but it also contains clusters of procedural rules. These procedural rules operate on the default and exception rules to establish and subsequently modify the superordinate and subordinate relationships among them and to make inferences.

Based on the auditor's observations and active goal of "determining the cause of the observed fluctuation," the superordinate and subordinate relationships or categories that are currently active in the auditor's mental model might include those pertaining to "SG&A expenses," "product mix," and "inherent risk." Associated with each of these categories are various attributes involving both observations from the current problem information (exception rules) and expectations generated from prior experiences (default rules). For example, under the inherent risk category, the following attributes may be encoded as exception rules: first-time audit of this client, a number of nonroutine transactions entered into by the client, and a highly turbulent industry. Other inherent-risk attributes that are not directly observed by the auditor in this situation but are generated as expectations (based on prior experience), would be encoded as default rules and may include the following: management integrity is questionable and management may be motivated to "cook the books." Relevant attributes also would be found under the "SG&A expenses" and "product mix" categories.

With the currently active mental model, the auditor next will make inferences in an attempt to solve the goal-directed problem of determining the cause of the observed fluctuations. Using the inferential rule of representativeness, the auditor first infers that the observed fluctuations in the client's account balances are likely due to financial statement error. Because the auditor has observed evidence that is highly representative of, or similar to, situations in which errors occur, he or she concludes that error must be present in the client's financial statements. The primary evidence on which this inference is based involves conditions consistent with high inherent risk (e.g., first-time audit of this client, a number of nonroutine transactions entered into by the client, and a highly turbulent industry). The auditor cannot be absolutely certain, however, that financial statement error is present. Although prior experience has shown that these inherent risk factors are very predictive of error, there is nevertheless variability in their strength, or predictive power. In addition, other problem information provides evidence suggesting that error may not have occurred (i.e., the client sold all of its foreign subsidiaries in the prior year).

Using the inferential rule of availability, the auditor next infers that the most likely cause of the observed fluctuations in the client's account balances is the specific financial statement error, "SG&A expenses and

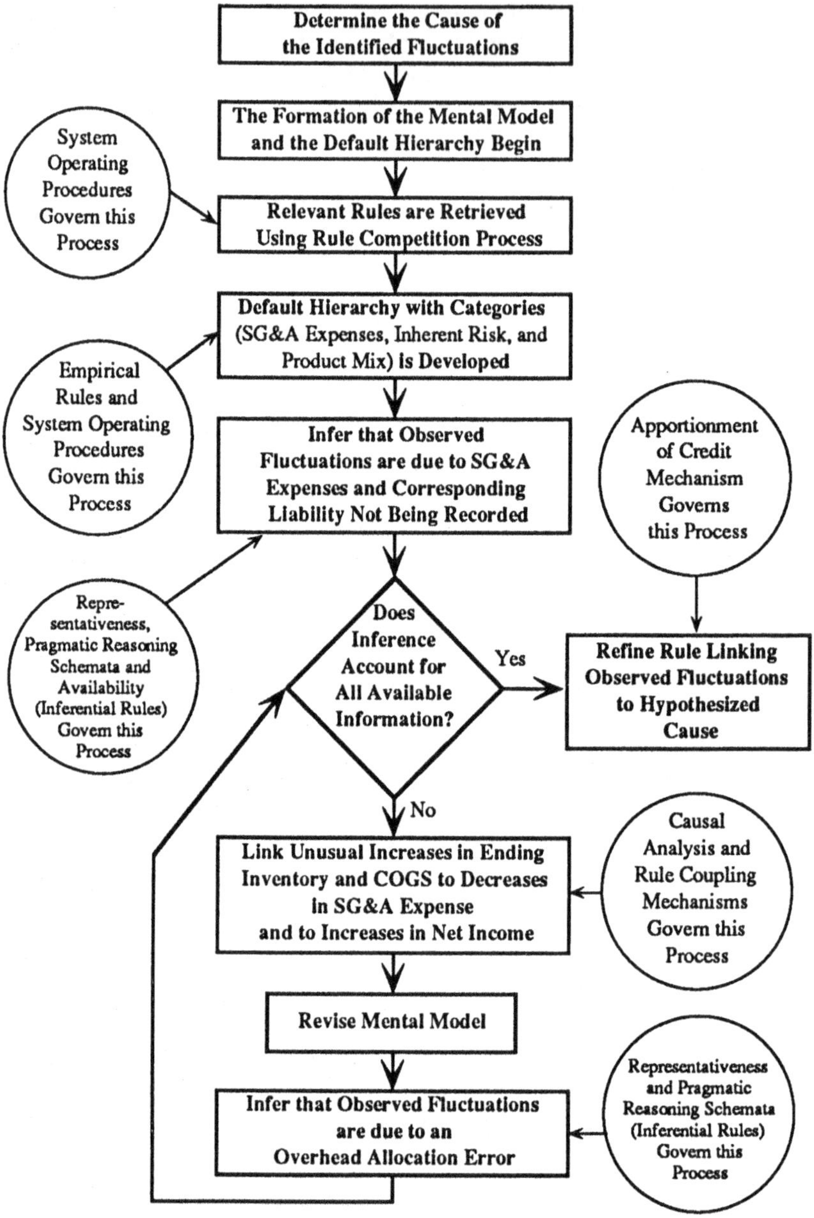

Figure 4. Audit example of the inductive inference process.

the corresponding liability not recorded." Because the auditor has recently experienced an audit in which this type of error was detected, this error is very salient in his or her memory and thus is easily recalled. Furthermore, using pragmatic reasoning schemata pertaining to the necessity and sufficiency of causes, the auditor also infers that one cause, not multiple causes, led to the observed fluctuations. Specifically, the dollar magnitude of the observed fluctuations (encoded as exception rules) and expectations about the typical dollar magnitude of various errors (encoded as default rules) lead to the inference that one cause is sufficient.

Next, to determine the accuracy of this tentative solution, a simulation is performed to determine whether it adequately accounts for the available problem information. Based on this analysis, the auditor concludes that the chosen error does not account for all of the observed fluctuations. Specifically, using the rule-refinement technique of causal analysis, the auditor realizes that two other components of the problem information--the unusual increases in the ending inventory and cost of goods sold--are not accounted for by the chosen error. Based on this failed problem solution, the auditor engages in the rule-generation technique of rule coupling to link the unusual increases in the ending inventory and cost of goods sold to the decrease in the SG&A expense and the increase in net income. The result of this rule-generation process is that the auditor's problem representation, or mental model, is now modified to incorporate the failed solution, include the additional problem information, and establish new linkages among this information.

Given the new mental model, the auditor again engages in induction to make inferences about the likely cause of the observed fluctuations. Using the inferential rule of representativeness and pragmatic reasoning schemata regarding necessity and sufficiency of causes, the auditor now infers that one cause, an overhead allocation error (SG&A costs that should have been expensed were incorrectly included in the cost of year-end inventory and in cost of goods sold) must have led to the fluctuations.

To determine the accuracy of this tentative solution to the problem, the auditor again engages in simulation to ascertain whether the solution adequately accounts for the available problem information. Based on this comparison, the auditor concludes that the chosen error does account for all of the observed fluctuations. Although uncertainty surrounding the validity of the chosen error remains, the auditor considers the reduction of uncertainty resulting from the additional "round" of induction sufficient for the purposes of ending the inductive-inference process and identifying a problem solution.

Future Research and Limitations

The model of professional audit judgment presented herein is hypothesized to be descriptive of the cognitive processes used by audit professionals.

Audit problem solving was broken down into four fundamental processes. First, goal development forms the basis for using specialized audit knowledge and directs problem representation and selection of the appropriate problem solution. Second, goal-relevant knowledge is retrieved to form the mental model, which is a cognitive representation of the audit problem. Third, inferences are generated to identify potential problem solutions. Fourth, rule refinement and rule generation are used if the mental model and its current inferences fail to adequately solve the audit problem.

The inductive model provides a comprehensive account of the cognitive processes underlying professional judgment in auditing. Although no existing audit studies have incorporated the inductive framework into their theoretical predictions, ex-post-analysis indicates that the findings of a number of audit studies are consistent with the cognitive theory of induction. Thus, this theory is useful because it provides a unifying framework for understanding extant research and, perhaps more importantly, for conducting future research. By examining the entire problem-solving process rather than concentrating on portions of that process, the theory enhances our understanding of audit expertise and the cognitive skills necessary to solve audit problems.

The inductive model provides a basis for conducting empirical research in a number of directions. First, the inductive theory provides insight into the structure and content of auditors' problem representations, or mental models, which are important to successful problem solving. Although some research has been conducted regarding the manner in which auditors represent audit problems, additional research is necessary to understand why different auditors may perceive the same problem information differently (i.e., why different auditors may develop different mental models). Such research is important since it will help to explain why one auditor may be able to correctly solve an audit problem while another auditor may be unable to do so. Since psychology research indicates that the quality, completeness, and coherence of the initial cognitive representation will determine the efficiency and effectiveness of further thinking (Glaser, 1984), such research may also help explain why different auditors may pursue different audit strategies. Second, the theory posits the importance of various inferential mechanisms in the problem-solving process. Research into the use of these mechanisms (in particular into the use of pragmatic reasoning schemata) offers an opportunity to study how auditors manipulate their knowledge and generate inferences from available problem information. Third, the theory provides a basis for investigating how auditors, in light of their experience and training, revise and add to their existing knowledge and bring that knowledge to bear in professional judgment situations. It is important to understand how the latter occurs, since audit expertise has been linked to the possession of a large body of audit knowledge, which can be successfully used in audit problem situations (Bonner & Lewis, 1991; Bonner, 1990; Davis & Solomon, 1989).

The cognitive theory of induction has at least two basic limitations. First, the theory does not capture the multiperson nature of auditing. As noted by Solomon (1987), much of auditing is performed in the context of audit teams, which are hierarchical working units comprised of auditors at various functional levels (i.e., staff, senior, manager, and engagement partner). Second, the theory ignores the strategic nature of the audit professional's relationship with the audit client (Anderson & Marchant, 1989). Both of these factors may influence the translation of professional audit judgments into action and thereby limit the model's ability to predict behavior. Despite these limitations, the model provides a constructive theoretical framework within which to study the psychology of professional judgment in auditing.

Endnotes

1. Other noncognitive factors that also are important to survival in the audit market include the ability to make justifiable/defensible judgments/decisions and the ability to attract and retain clients (Davis & Solomon, 1989).

2. As noted by Davis and Solomon (1989), there is no timely revelation of an outcome referent for many audit tasks. Consequently, the auditor's ability to learn from outcome feedback may be more inhibited in the audit domain than in other professional settings. However, in light of the formal audit review process in which superiors on the audit team review, or critically evaluate, the work of subordinates (Solomon, 1987), the auditor would be expected to receive process feedback for most audit tasks.

3. Inductions typically are limited to situations in which an individual does not know what to do next or when an expectation or prediction has failed. For example, an auditor would make no inference from the observation that the client writes checks (rather than paying in cash) for purchases of goods and services. In this case, no expectations were disconfirmed by the observation nor was the accomplishment of any goals thwarted.

4. Abduction also can occur when explanatory hypotheses are generated from long-term memory in response to an unusual problem situation. For example, when an auditor performs an analytical review, he or she must generate potential explanatory hypotheses in response to an observed fluctuation in an account balance or financial ratio. Such hypotheses are typically generated from long-term memory and thus do not trigger a new generalization. Consequently, this type of abduction cannot be considered to involve rule generation.

4
A Review of Audit Research Using the Belief-Adjustment Model

Stephen K. Asare and William F. Messier, Jr.

Introduction

The basic audit process requires that the auditor search for and evaluate evidence related to an audit assertion (e.g., Cushing & Loebbecke, 1986; Felix & Kinney, 1982; Gibbins, 1984; Knechel & Messier, 1990). In evaluating an audit assertion (e.g., validity of accounts receivable balance), the auditor begins with an initial belief and then revises that belief upward or downward depending on whether each new piece of evidence is positive or negative, respectively. While this process has been modeled using Bayes rule (Kinney, 1975), a number of behavioral studies in auditing (e.g., Joyce & Biddle, 1981a, b; Kinney & Uecker, 1982; and others) indicate that Bayes rule is not a good descriptor of the auditor's judgment process. In particular, the research results have indicated that an auditor's judgment process is sensitive to normatively irrelevant variables such as hypothesis frame (Kida, 1984b), temporal sequence (Joyce & Biddle, 1981a), and more generally that auditors employ heuristics in their judgments of probability. These findings are consistent with similar research in psychology (e.g., Slovic & Lichtenstein, 1971; Tversky & Kahneman, 1974). Accordingly, decision theorists have recently focused on the effects of task variables on information-processing strategies. This line of research aims at developing a "procedural theory of judgment" that accounts for the sensitivity of decision behavior to environmental changes (Hogarth & Einhorn, 1990; Lopes, 1982; and others).

Following this approach, Hogarth and Einhorn (1990) have developed a descriptive model of the belief revision process, which takes into account a number of task variables (e.g., order of evidence and response mode) that previous psychological research indicates affect belief revisions. Their model is referred to as the *belief-adjustment* model[1] and it "presumes a simple information-processing strategy, [and] its interaction with these different task variables yields a complex pattern of predictions concerning order effects" (p. 3).

From an auditing perspective, order effects have potential implications for the efficiency and effectiveness of the audit (Ashton & Ashton, 1988). Efficiency can be affected since the order in which evidence is processed may limit or extend the auditor's search for additional evidence. This may have an impact on the cost and timeliness of an audit. From an effectiveness perspective, order effects may lead auditors to choose different audit actions, which in turn may reduce audit accuracy (i.e., less consensus).

Auditing researchers have examined the belief-adjustment model because it provides a good descriptive model of the auditor's judgment process. In this chapter we review the auditing studies that have used the belief adjustment model as a framework for examining auditors' judgments. The remainder of the chapter proceeds as follows. In the next section we summarize the belief-adjustment model as proposed by Hogarth and Einhorn (1990) and explain its predictions. The following section reviews the audit research on the model. The last sections provide directions for future research and concluding comments.

The Belief-Adjustment Model

Overview

The belief-adjustment model posits that individuals revise their beliefs using a sequential anchoring-and-adjustment strategy where an initial belief, or anchor, is adjusted by subsequent pieces of evidence. The model's descriptive appeal lies in its cognitive economy since (unlike Bayes theorem) it allows the decision maker to evaluate evidence with respect to a single hypothesis under consideration. The model is formalized as follows:

$$S_k = S_{k-1} + w_k[s(x_k) - R] \quad (1)$$

where S_k = degree of belief in some hypothesis after evaluating k pieces of evidence ($0 \leq S_k \leq 1$);

S_{k-1} = the anchor or prior opinion and the initial strength of belief is denoted S_0;

$s(x_k)$ = subjective evaluation of the kth piece of evidence (bounds on the magnitude of $s(x_k)$ are specified later);

R	=	the reference point or background against which the impact of the kth piece of evidence is evaluated;
w_k	=	the adjustment weight for the kth piece of evidence.

The first term on the right denotes the anchor while the second term denotes the adjustment to the anchor. The model includes three subprocesses: (a) evidence encoding, (b) evidence processing, and (c) adjustment mechanisms.

Encoding. Hogarth and Einhorn (1990) model the encoding of new evidence as $[s(x_k)-R]$. In this formulation, the impact of new evidence is the difference between an individual's subjective evaluation of evidence and a reference point. Hogarth and Einhorn (1990) adopt the position that encoding reflects the purpose of belief revision, and they distinguish between evaluation and estimation tasks. In evaluation tasks, evidence is encoded as positive or negative relative to a causal hypothesis. The implication is that evidence is seen as bipolar such that $-1 \leq s(x_k) \leq +1$ and $R = 0$. In this case, Equation 1 takes the following form

$$S_k = S_{k-1} + w_k s(x_k). \tag{2}$$

On the other hand, the objective of an estimation task is to assess some type of moving average. In such tasks, the individual is hypothesized to be sensitive to the difference between the current anchor (S_{k-1}) and the level of opinion suggested by the evidence being integrated. As an estimate, this implies that evidence is unipolar such that $0 \leq s(x_k) \leq +1$ and $R = S_{k-1}$. In this case, Equation 1 takes the following form

$$S_k = S_{k-1} + w_k [s(x_k) - S_{k-1}], \tag{3}$$

which after rearranging terms leads to

$$S_k = (1 - w_k) S_{k-1} + w_k s(x_k). \tag{4}$$

Hogarth and Einhorn (1990) point out that while evaluation (Equation 2) and estimation (Equation 3) rely on an anchoring-and-adjustment strategy, the data generated by each subprocess will fit an additive and averaging model, respectively. Because of the nature of auditing, we suspect that many audit tasks involve an evaluation subprocess. First, the outcomes of most audit tasks involve judgments on dichotomous scales (i.e., the audit objective is met or not met) as opposed to estimates on a continuous scale, which are typical of estimation tasks. Second, the evidence auditors examine is bipolar (positive or negative) as opposed to unipolar.

Processing. In the previous discussion $s(x_k)$ was represented as a single piece of evidence. This formulation assumes that evidence is processed in a step-by-step (SbS) fashion. However, Hogarth and Einhorn (1990) also allow $[s(x_k) - R]$ to represent the net impact of several pieces of evidence. This latter formulation provides for an end-of-sequence (EoS) process. With an SbS process the individual adjusts his or her belief as each piece of evidence is processed. The EoS process assumes that the individual adjusts the initial belief by the net effect of the sequence of evidence. The EoS strategy is represented by

$$S_k = S_0 + w_k [s(x_1, \ldots, x_k) - R], \tag{5}$$

where $s(x_1, \ldots, x_k)$ is some function (e.g., weighted average) of the subjective evaluations of each piece of evidence in the sequence.

Adjustment. According to the model, adjusting beliefs to the impact of new evidence reflects a trade-off between adaptation and inertia. Individuals are hypothesized to adjust their beliefs to adapt to new evidence; however, such adaptation to evidence does not proceed at the same rate over time, nor is it independent of the sign of the adjustment.

To model the adaptation process, Hogarth and Einhorn (1990) hypothesize that the adjustment weight, w_k, depends on both the sign of the impact of the evidence, i.e., of $[s(x_k) - R]$, and the level of the anchor, S_{k-1}. Adaptation is modeled by assuming a contrast effect. Specifically, Hogarth and Einhorn (1990) argue that for $s(x_k) \leq R$ the adjustment weight should be proportional to S_{k-1}. Their rationale is that if the current position (the anchor) concerning a hypothesis is strong and a strong piece of negative evidence is received, the downward belief revision will be larger than if the current position was weak. Conversely, when $s(x_k) > R$, the adjustment weight is inversely proportional to the anchor. This specification leads to

$$w_k = \alpha S_{k-1} \text{ when } s(x_k) \leq R \tag{6a}$$

and

$$w_k = \beta(1 - S_{k-1}) \text{ when } s(x_k) > R, \tag{6b}$$

where α and β are constants such that $0 \leq \alpha, \beta \leq 1$. The constants α and β capture the individual's sensitivity towards negative and positive evidence, respectively. Low (high) values of α and β specify low (high) sensitivity to new evidence. Over time the values for α and β are expected to decline. To complete the model, Equations 6a and 6b are substituted into equation 1 which yields

$$S_k = S_{k-1} + \alpha S_{k-1}[s(x_k) - R] \quad \text{for } s(x_k) \leq R \tag{7a}$$

and

$$S_k = S_{k-1} + \beta(1 - S_{k-1})[s(x_k) - R] \quad \text{for } s(x_k) > R. \tag{7b}$$

In this form, the degree of belief in a hypothesis is a function of the anchor, the sequence of the evidence received, how the evidence is encoded, and the sensitivity to positive and negative evidence.

Model Predictions

Figure 1 presents the predictions of the belief-adjustment model for an SbS or EoS process and categorizes them by the complexity of the evidence and length of series. Additionally, this figure distinguishes between models where $R = 0$ or S_{k-1}.

Here, we limit our discussions of the model's predictions to evaluation-type tasks ($-1 \leq s(x_k) \leq +1$ and $R = 0$), a short series of evidence, and the SbS process. This approach is taken because we believe
that it is most representative of the audit process and it is consistent with the vast majority of the empirical work in auditing using the model. The reader is referred to Hogarth and Einhorn (1990) for details on the development of the other predictions.

For short series of evidence, the model predicts no effect for consistent evidence when $R = 0$. To show this for negative evidence, Equation 7a can be rewritten as

$$S_k = S_{k-1}[1 + \alpha s(x_k)]. \tag{8}$$

Encoding	$R = S_{k-1}$		$R = 0$			
Type of Evidence	All		Mixed		Consistent	
Response Mode	EoS	SbS	EoS	SbS	EoS	SbS
Short Series						
Simple	Primacy	Primacy	Primacy	Recency	Primacy	No effect
Complex	Recency	Recency	Recency	Recency	No effect	No effect
Long Series	Force towards primacy	Force towards primacy	Force towards primacy	Force towards primacy	Primacy	Primacy

Figure 1. Predictions of the belief-adjustment model*

For two pieces of negative evidence (k = 2), Equation 8 can be expanded to

$$S_2 = S_0[1 + \alpha s(x_1)][1 + \alpha s(x_2)]. \tag{9}$$

Since multiplication is commutative, S_2 is not affected by the order in which $s(x_1)$ and $s(x_2)$ are processed.

For positive evidence, Equation 7b can be rewritten as

$$S_k = S_{k-1}[1 - \beta s(x_k)] + \beta s(x_k). \tag{10}$$

When $k = 2$, Equation 10 can be expanded to

$$S_2 = S_0 + \beta(1 - S_0)[s(x_1) + s(x_2) - \beta s(x_1)s(x_2)]. \tag{11}$$

Again, both addition and multiplication are commutative, and the order in which $s(x_1)$ and $s(x_2)$ are evaluated has no effect.

For mixed evidence, the model predicts recency. To understand why this occurs, consider the effects of processing a negative piece of evidence, denoted $s(x_-)$, followed by a positive piece, denoted $s(x_+)$, and then the processing of the positive piece followed by the negative piece. In this case an order effect can be defined as

$$D = S(-,+) - S(+,-), \tag{12}$$

*Hogarth and Einhorn, 1990, p. 66. Adapted with permission.

where D is the difference between the final belief revisions for each order. Using Equations 7a and 7b, this can be rewritten as

$$D = [S_0 + w_1[s(x_-) + r_2 s(x_+)] - [S_0 + r_1 s(x_+) + w_2 s(x_-)]$$

$$= s(x_+)\,(r_2 - r_1) + s(x_-)(w_2 - w_1), \tag{13}$$

where $r_1 = ß(1 - S_0)$, $r_2 = ß[1 - \{S_0 + w_1 s(x_-)\}]$, $w_1 = \alpha S_0$ and $w_2 = \alpha[S_0 + r_1 s(x_+)]$.

In this case, $(r_2 - r_1) = -S_0\alpha ß s(x_-)$ and $(w_2 - w_1) = -(1 - S_0)\alpha ß s(x_+)$. Substituting these values into Equation 13 yields

$$D = -s(x_+)S_0\alpha ß s(x_-) - s(x_-)(1 - S_0)\alpha ß s(x_+)$$

$$= -\alpha ß s(x_-)s(x_+) > 0 \tag{14}$$

because $s(x_-) < 0$.

Since D is positive, recency occurs and is the product of both the sensitivity to evidence and the subjective strengths of the evidence. This also shows that S_0, the initial belief, has no impact on the size of the recency effect.

These predictions hold for short series of evidence. With longer series of evidence, Hogarth and Einhorn (1990) assume that α and ß will decline over time and the model will predict primacy for consistent evidence and a force towards primacy for mixed evidence. In developing the belief-adjustment model, Hogarth and Einhorn (1990) reviewed nearly 60 psychological studies where order-effects were found. These studies were classified along three dimensions: complexity of the evidence, length of the series of evidence, and response mode. Complexity is an increasing function of the amount of evidence that needs to be processed at each judgment and the lack of familiarity with the task. Length of the series of evidence relates to the number of pieces of evidence that must be evaluated. Hogarth and Einhorn (1990) classified short series as containing 2 to 12 pieces of evidence, while a long series contained over 20 items. Response mode included the SbS and EoS processes described earlier. The predictions of the belief-adjustment model are consistent with Hogarth and Einhorn's analysis of previous psychological studies on order effects and response mode.

Review of Relevant Literature

In this section we will first review the basic experiments conducted by Hogarth and Einhorn (1990). We will then review the audit-related studies[2]. Hogarth and Einhorn's empirical work is reviewed in some detail since most of the accounting studies have followed their basic approach. Our review is limited to published papers and working papers that we identified in a limited survey.

The Einhorn and Hogarth Study

In a series of five experiments, Hogarth and Einhorn (1990) tested the belief-adjustment model's predictions concerning order effects. Experiments 1 to 4 tested order effects for complex stimuli involving a short series of evidence assuming $R = 0$. The subjects judged the likelihood of a causal hypothesis in each of four scenarios: (a) a defective stereo speaker thought to have a bad connection, (b) a baseball player whose hitting had improved dramatically after a new coaching program, (c) an increase in sales of a supermarket product following an advertising campaign, and (d) the contraction of lung cancer by a worker in a chemical factory. Each scenario involved an initial description (the anchor) and additional pieces of information presented on separate pages (SbS) or on one page (EoS). After reading the stem (anchor), subjects were asked to rate the likelihood that the suspected factor was the cause of the outcome on a rating scale from 0 to 100. After responding to this question, subjects turned the page(s) of their experimental booklets and were presented with the additional pieces of evidence.

The results for Experiments 1 to 4 supported the model's predictions of no order effects for consistent evidence and recency effects for mixed evidence. Moreover, the order effects held across both the SbS and EoS response modes. In Experiment 5, Hogarth and Einhorn (1990) tried to rule out alternative explanations for the results in Experiments 1 and 2. They designed an experiment where consistent evidence was presented in alternative forms that would result in either an evaluation or estimation strategy. They hypothesized that the use of the estimation strategy would lead to a recency effect. The results showed no recency for the evaluation strategy and a recency effect for the estimation strategy. These findings reinforce the results of Experiments 1 and 2.

Audit-Related Studies

Auditing researchers have tested the belief adjustment in a number of different audit settings. The early research focused on basic predictions of the model related to order and response mode effects. Later work has examined whether the reported recency effects had an impact on the efficiency or effectiveness of the auditor's judgment process and whether certain institutional factors may mitigate order effects.

Audit Studies on the Model's Predictions. Ashton and Ashton (1988) conducted five experiments using 211 auditors to test the predictions of the model. These auditors had a mean experience level of three years in public accounting. In the first two experiments (1A and 1B), subjects were asked to assume that they were investigating the payroll records of an audit client and were further told that a preliminary investigation of internal controls over payroll indicated that the likelihood the controls would prevent or detect material errors was either .20, .50, or .80. These initial estimates were meant to serve as anchors, which were updated sequentially by pieces of either positive or negative evidence. Experiment 1A (1B) contained four pieces of positive (negative) evidence. The additional pieces of evidence were presented in two orders: two pieces of strong positive (negative) evidence followed by two pieces of weak positive (negative) evidence. After each piece of evidence was presented, the auditors were asked to judge the likelihood that the system would prevent or detect a material error. Subjects responded by marking an "X" on a line numbered from 0 to 100. The dependent variable was the change in the likelihood rating ($S_4 - S_0$).

In experiments 2A and 2B, the principal issue studied was the prediction of recency effects in the sequential evaluation of mixed evidence. The design was identical to the earlier experiments except that the sequence of evidence contained two pieces of strong positive evidence and two pieces of strong negative evidence. The order of the evidence was: (+ + − −) or (− − + +). Experiment 2A involved a payroll scenario while experiment 2B contained an accounts receivable scenario.

Experiment 3 examined the impact of presentation mode on the belief revision process. Two presentation modes were tested: SbS and EoS. Ashton and Ashton's tests were based on the contrast/surprise version (Einhorn & Hogarth, 1985) of the model. Given certain assumptions about the auditor's attitude toward evidence, the model predicted that a "dilution" effect would occur; that is, simultaneous processing of evidence would lead to less extreme belief revisions than sequential processing of the same evidence.

The results of the Ashton and Ashton (1988) study for experiments 1A and 1B are consistent with the model's prediction of no order effects for consistent evidence. In addition, they reported evidence that supported the model's assumption that smaller (larger) anchors are adjusted upward (downward) more by positive (negative) evidence. For instance, for subjects who received consistent negative evidence with anchors of .20, .50, and .80, mean belief change was −.077, −.228, and −.361, respectively.

The results for experiments 2A and 2B show a recency effect as predicted by the model. For example, in experiment 2A, the auditor's mean belief change in + + − − (− − + +) order was −.070 (.002). Similar results were reported for experiment 2B. In addition, a significant main effect was found for the size of the initial anchor consistent with the contrast assumption of the model. Results of experiment 3 indicated that given the same pieces of evidence, simultaneous processing of evidence led to a smaller belief revision than sequential processing. This finding was interpreted as being consistent with the analytical results of Einhorn and Hogarth (1985), which predicted a dilution effect for simultaneous processing of evidence. In turn, this dilution effect was attributed to auditors being prone to revise their beliefs when new evidence is received and being more sensitive to negative evidence.

While Ashton and Ashton (1988) used "simplified, well-defined settings," Tubbs, Messier and Knechel (1990) used scenarios that were more complex and closer to actual auditing contexts. They conducted four experiments using 250 auditors to test the order and response mode predictions of the model. Subjects in the study were audit seniors with three years experience. Two tasks were employed in the study: an accounts receivable scenario dealing with the collectibility of a major account and an accounts payable scenario dealing with the probability that accounts payable are fairly stated. Two response modes were tested: an SbS mode in which judgments were elicited after each piece of new evidence and an EoS mode in which judgments were elicited after all information had been presented. Experiments 1 and 2 included two pieces of consistent evidence. Experiment 3 included two pieces of mixed evidence, while experiment 4 included four pieces of mixed evidence.

The results indicated no order effects for consistent positive or negative evidence. In experiment 3, when two pieces of mixed evidence were evaluated, the predicted recency effect occurred only in the SbS response mode. When four pieces of mixed evidence were evaluated, recency occurred in both response modes. Thus, with the one exception, the results support the model's predictions.

Bonner and Butler (1989) tested the predictions of the model using an analytical procedures task. They conducted three experiments that involved 311 auditors with an average experience level of 3.56 years. Experiments 1 and 2 tested the model's predictions using four pieces of consistent positive and negative evidence, respectively. Experiment 3 included four pieces of mixed evidence.

Contrary to the model's prediction, an order effect was reported in experiment 1 when consistent positive evidence was presented sequentially. However, no order effect was found for simultaneous processing. Moreover, the simultaneous response mode resulted in more extreme belief revision than sequential processing, but only in one of the two order conditions. Mixed results also were reported for experiment 2. Consistent with the model's predictions, no order effects were found in negative evidence, but contrary to the model's predictions, no dilution effects were found for either sequential or simultaneous processing of evidence. Finally, in experiment 3 no recency effects were detected when the auditors evaluated mixed evidence. Bonner and Butler (1989) attribute the finding of no recency effect for mixed evidence to the auditors not being able "to detect that the pattern of ratio fluctuations was inconsistent with the hypothesized error . . ."(p. 20).

Koch, Pei, and Reed (1989) tested the predictions of the model in a performance auditing setting. They argued that the decision environment faced by state auditors is less prone to litigation and that evidence used for performance audits is often low in diagnosticity. The effect of these two factors may lead state auditors' attitude toward evidence to differ from that of financial auditors. Given that the recency effects predicted by the belief adjustment model is partly determined by attitudes toward evidence, their study examines whether the recency effects reported in the financial audit settings generalize to a performance audit setting.

In their experiment, 35 state auditors with an average of 5.50 years of experience were asked to evaluate the efficiency and effectiveness of a state program established to reduce state welfare rolls. Each subject examined two case scenarios—an efficiency audit and an effectiveness audit. For the efficiency audit, the auditors were told that performance of the state program should be evaluated by four types of output services. The effectiveness audit was evaluated by four types of impact measures. Each piece of evidence related to one of these measures and was manipulated by setting its value at the office's expected performance plus (for positive) or minus (for negative) 2 standard deviations.

Subjects were provided with background data for each audit. After reviewing the background data, the auditors provided an initial assessment on a 0 to 100 point scale of the performance of that office. They were then presented with the four pieces of additional evidence and asked to revise their assessment after each piece of evidence.

Koch et al. (1989) examined three variables: order of evidence, type of task (efficiency versus effectiveness audit), and serial position. Order of presentation was manipulated in the usual manner. Serial position was manipulated to address the possibility that auditors' sensitivity toward evidence may decline with the length of evidence. This manipulation was achieved by presenting evidence to half of the subjects in one sequence and reversing the sequence for the other half of the subjects.

The results indicated that there was a significant recency effect. However, the state auditors belief adjustments were more affected by positive evidence than negative evidence. This is the opposite of the findings of Ashton and Ashton (1988) and Tubbs et al. (1990) and corroborates the conjecture of Ashton and Ashton (1990) that auditors' sensitivity toward negative evidence is shaped by their legal and professional environment.

While the belief adjustment model predicts a recency effect in belief revision, other psychological theories of updating suggest a more complex set of predictions. In particular, the literature on confirmation bias (Church, 1990) suggests that subjects have a tendency to overweight evidence that supports their initial beliefs and to discount or underweight evidence that is not consistent with those initial beliefs. If auditors' judgments are prone to this confirmation bias then it would be expected that evidence that supports initial beliefs would have a stronger impact regardless of the sequence. In effect, positive evidence would have a stronger impact when the initial beliefs are high and negative evidence would have a stronger impact when the initial beliefs are low; this is a pattern of prediction that is counter to the contrast effect predicted by the belief-adjustment model.

Butt and Campbell (1989) examined this issue in a study that manipulated prior beliefs, hypothesis-testing strategy and order of evidence. The subjects were 123 auditors and the task was to evaluate the likelihood that the internal control structure would prevent or detect a material error. The auditors were provided with background information about the control structure and the past audit record of a hypothetical manufacturing firm. Following this information, the auditors received ten pieces of information about specific controls (five positive and five negative) and made three likelihood judgments. The first likelihood judgment was made after the background information and the other two likelihood judgments were made after evaluating the fifth and tenth pieces of evidence, respectively.

Prior beliefs were manipulated by varying the background material between subjects. One treatment consisted of a positive (negative) evaluation of the company (i.e., the company had received a positive (negative) evaluation of controls in the past). Order was manipulated by presenting the ten pieces of information in one of two orders: five positive items followed by five negative items or the five negative items followed by the five positive items. Finally, the hypothesis-testing strategy was manipulated by reminding the auditors, prior to being presented with the ten pieces of information, that they were looking for evidence that confirms (disconfirms) their beliefs about the strength of internal control structure.

The results indicated marginally significant recency effects for subjects in the low priors condition but no order effects were observed for subjects in the high priors condition[3]. Their results also suggested that auditors are not prone to a confirmation bias regardless of their initial beliefs.

Order Effects and Audit Effectiveness. Given the pervasiveness of recency effects in auditors' judgments, there is concern over its effect on the efficiency and effectiveness of an audit. Tubbs et al. (1990, p. 459) suggest that recency effects may lead to different levels of testing or different types of audit reports. Two studies (Asare, 1990; Messier, 1990) have addressed the question of whether recency effects also result in different actions on the part of auditors.

Asare (1990) examined this issue in a task involving the choice of audit reports. He hypothesized that in choosing an audit report an auditor would compare his or her likelihood rating of a firm's going-concern status $[P(C|E)]$ to his or her threshold for issuing a going-concern report $[P^*(C)]$. If $P(C|E)$ is $\leq P^*(C)$, the auditor will issue a modified report, otherwise he or she would issue an unqualified report. He argued that $P(C|E)$ is reached via a sequential process, which allows for cognitive economy but is subject to the recency effects reported in earlier studies. Thus, after controlling for $P^*(C)$, any observed recency effects in $P(C|E)$ should translate into the choice of different audit reports. Specifically, Asare argued that subjects who evaluated contrary information followed by mitigating factors will issue more unqualified opinions than those auditors who evaluate mitigating factors followed by contrary information.

Two experiments were conducted involving 100 managers and partners, working on an actual audit case obtained from the files of a Big-Six CPA firm. The subjects were randomly assigned to either a viability or a failure hypothesis frame and made an initial assessment of $P(C|E)$ based on the client's financial statements. Subjects next updated this anchor with two pieces of contrary information and two pieces of mitigating factors. The order of evidence was manipulated in the usual way. Finally, subjects provided their threshold levels $[P^*(C)]$ for issuing a going-concern report and made a reporting choice. After controlling for $P^*(C)$, Asare reports that recency effects occurred in both the likelihood ratings and the opinion choices of the subjects. Moreover, this recency effect occurred irrespective of subjects' hypothesis frame. Asare suggested that since audit actions were systematically affected by order, the order in which evidence is received by an auditor affects audit consensus.

Messier (1990) also examined the issue of whether recency effects lead to different actions by auditors. He examined this issue in two experiments involving an accounts payable scenario and a going-concern scenario. This allowed him to test the effect of recency on the extent of audit testing and audit report formulation.

Fifty auditors with 2.5 years of experience took part in experiment 1 (accounts payable). The auditors were presented with a basic case scenario, which included an audit budget, and then received four pieces of mixed evidence in an SbS response mode. Each piece of evidence included the actual audit hours to perform the procedure. For positive evidence the actual audit hours equaled the budgeted hours. For the negative evidence the actual hours exceeded the budgeted hours by 50 percent. The auditors provided likelihood judgments about whether accounts payable were fairly presented on a 0 to 100 scale. After making the likelihood judgments, the auditors were asked to provide additional audit procedures that needed to be conducted and estimated audit hours for each procedure. Order effects were tested using the change in beliefs ($S_4 - S_0$). The dependent measure for the extent of testing was the total additional audit hours.

Experiment 2 examined the same issues as experiment 1 except it used a more complex problem domain: going concern. A case was developed based on a NASDAQ company that had just received a going-concern modification. The basic company scenario was followed by two pieces of mitigating (positive) and two pieces of contrary (negative) evidence. Eighteen partners and 31 managers, with average experience levels of 17.3 and 7.9 years, respectively, participated in the experiment. The auditors provided a likelihood judgment about going concern using an SbS response mode. They also provided a likelihood judgment on whether they would issue a modified report.[4]

The results in Experiment 1 showed a recency effect, but there was no difference in the audit hours budgeted by the auditors across the two orders of evidence. This result suggests that recency occurred but that it did not affect the extent of testing. A recency effect in the likelihood rating on going-concern also was found in experiment 2. The auditors' likelihood judgments about issuing a modified report also were significantly different across orders of evidence. This result suggests that the recency effect affected the auditors' report choice. However, since the average likelihood for issuing a modified report was so high relative to Asare's $P^*(C)$, Messier (1990) concluded that from a practical point of view most auditors would have issued a modified report. Thus, Messier concludes that recency occurs in likelihood ratings but does not affect the extent of testing or report formulation.

Mitigating Order Effects. Messier and Tubbs (1990) suggest that such recency effects might be mitigated by mechanisms that exist in the audit process. They hypothesized that the review of audit work by more experienced auditors would mitigate recency effects. Messier and Tubbs (1990) argue that a more experienced auditor would have more confidence in his or her assessment of the problem and thus would be less sensitive toward positive or negative evidence (i.e., α and β). When a more experienced auditor reviews the work of a subordinate, his or her judgment may be affected by the perceived reliability of the subordinate (Bamber, 1983). Messier and Tubbs (1990) tested two hypotheses: (a) more experienced auditors (reviewers and managers) will exhibit less recency than the inexperienced auditors (H1), and (b) the managers will exhibit less recency than the reviewers (H2).

Messier and Tubbs (1990) tested these hypotheses as follows: The subjects from the EoS response mode in experiment 4 of the Tubbs et al. (1990) study were used as the less experienced auditors. Seventy-two manager-level auditors were assigned to one of two conditions. In the first condition (reviewers) the managers reviewed the judgments of a reliable senior on the accounts receivable scenario used in experiment 4 of Tubbs et al. (1990). The values provided to the managers with each piece of evidence were the average likelihoods of the auditors in that experiment for each order of evidence. The managers provided an initial assessment of the case (S_0) and a final likelihood after reviewing the judgments of the senior (S_4). The second condition (managers) simply had the managers complete the instrument in the same way as the seniors in Tubbs et al. (1990).

The results of testing H1 showed that the hypothesized effect only occurred in the (+ + − −) order condition. It appears that the less experienced auditors tend to overreact more than the more experienced auditors when negative evidence follows positive evidence. H2 was tested by testing the following contrast: recency effect (reviewers) > recency effect (managers). This contrast was not significant. Given the result for H1, Messier and Tubbs (1990) concluded that recency is mitigated by experience and possibly by the review process.

Areas for Future Research

It is apparent from the preceding discussion of the belief-adjustment model and the review of the empirical data that the model has an intuitive and predictive appeal as a descriptive model of the auditor's belief revision process. Given that belief updating is an important component of the audit process, it appears the model can be used as a theoretical framework to address several audit-related issues. In this section, we focus on areas where the model could be used for further theoretical and empirical work.

One important and unexplored area concerns how the order in which evidence is received affects the amount of evidence collected to support the audit opinion. Recall that the paradigmatic approach employed in all the prior studies was to present the auditors with evidence and observe how manipulation of the response mode and the temporal sequence have an impact upon their likelihood ratings. Such an approach ignores the information search activities of auditors, thereby imposing artificial structure on the audit task (Einhorn & Hogarth 1981). In this regard an important research question involves how the first piece of evidence affects the amount of evidence collected. For instance, do auditors who receive negative (positive) evidence prematurely terminate their evidence search activities and reject (accept) the assertions of the client? Research along these lines would be extremely useful since the auditor's information search activities have an impact directly on the cost and timeliness of the audit. (See Knechel & Messier, 1990, for a study that looks at auditors' information choice decisions.)

Another area that deserves research attention is the effect of institutional variables on auditors' belief updating and the predictions of the belief-adjustment model. The studies that have been conducted to date omit several important institutional variables presumably to enhance internal validity. In particular, subjects' decisions are (a) not reviewed by their superiors, (b) provided no explicit incentives, (c) not required to justify their decisions, and (d) the decisions made under time pressure. These institutional variables may eliminate the order and response mode effects reported in these studies. For example, Tetlock (1983) has shown that holding subjects accountable for their judgments eliminates primacy effects. Whether these omitted characteristics of the audit task setting affect the belief updating process is not known and remains a fruitful avenue for future research.

Another area where the belief-adjustment model can offer important insights is the nature of expertise in audit judgment (Ashton & Ashton 1988; Messier & Tubbs, 1990). These insights could be obtained by focusing attention on the sensitivity parameters incorporated in the model. Recall that the model distinguishes between sensitivity toward positive and negative evidence and is able to model asymmetric attitudes toward evidence. Thus, one way of understanding the nature of audit expertise is to examine whether auditors display differential sensitivity to positive and negative evidence, and whether auditors' attitude toward evidence differs from other groups. Ashton and Ashton (1990) have argued that the legal and professional environment in which auditors work may lead them to have evidence attitudes that differ from other groups. Research that explicitly measures the α and β parameters of the belief adjustment model would complement their results. On a prescriptive note, research could proceed by determining the appropriate levels of sensitivity toward evidence.

The process by which auditors encode evidence prior to belief updating needs to be studied. In all the studies that we reviewed it was assumed that evidence is coded "correctly" (consistent with the researcher expectations) by the auditor. However, the encoding process is likely to be affected by the auditor's previous experience, ambiguity of the evidence, and dependencies among different pieces of evidence. To illustrate this problem, consider experiment 1B in Ashton and Ashton (1988). Subjects were told that the likelihood that the internal controls would prevent or detect material errors is .20 and received four additional pieces of negative (positive) evidence. It is likely that subjects would perceive the additional pieces of evidence as redundant since the anchor of .20 would lead them to ignore controls and go directly to substantive testing. We believe the encoding process is critical to belief updating and is in need of further research.

Finally, Asare (1990) concluded that order effects have an impact on the auditors' actions. Messier (1990) reports that the recency effects did not affect the extent of audit testing or report formulation (but, see endnote 4). Future research should reconcile these divergent findings.

Concluding Comment

In conclusion, we believe that the belief-adjustment model has an intuitive appeal and the empirical work that has been done so far barely scratches the surface of several issues that could be addressed with the model.

Endnotes

1. Earlier versions of this model had different functional forms and were referred to as the contrast-surprise model (Einhorn & Hogarth, 1985) and the contract-inertia model (Einhorn & Hogarth, 1988). The predictions of these earlier models are consistent with the predictions from the belief-adjustment model.

2. There has been additional research (Dillard, Kauffman & Spires, 1989) on the belief-adjustment model in other functional areas (e.g., management accounting) of accounting.

3. While the study is interesting because it attempted to specify in more detail the conditions under which order effects occur, there are two problems that limit its usefulness in terms of providing evidence on the belief-adjustment model. First, the response mode used in the experiment is consistent neither with the EoS or SbS sequence as described by Hogarth and Einhorn (1990). Second, the rating scale used by Butt and Campbell (1989) was such that positive information was confirming for auditors with high priors but disconfirming for auditors with low priors. This is not consistent with the belief-adjustment model where evidence is encoded with respect to a hypothesis regardless of the level of beliefs in that hypothesis (Hogarth and Einhorn, 1990).

4. It would have been more appropriate to have asked the auditors to provide a choice of reports rather than a likelihood. See Messier (1990) for further discussion of this issue.

5
Using Experimental Economics in Auditing Research

Ronald King*

Introduction

My objective in this chapter is threefold: (a) to provide a brief overview of the basic features of the experimental economics paradigm, (b) to review some of the auditing research that has used this paradigm, and (c) to offer some possibilities for future research, with an emphasis on identifying issues that might encourage the integration of experimental economics and behavioral auditing research. Experimental economics refers to a research paradigm that uses controlled laboratory conditions to investigate the relative predictive ability of economic theories. Implicit in the approach is a focus on how individual behavior is influenced by economic markets and institutions.[1] The impetus to investigate how, and to what extent, economic institutions and markets effect individual behavior stems in part from the results of behavioral research.

The behavioral research paradigm shares with the experimental economics paradigm an emphasis on data collection for the purposes of scientific investigation. Both paradigms are concerned with the "theory-data feedback process" (iterative development of theory and data collection) with the goal of improving the understanding and prediction of phenomena that occur in natural settings. The two paradigms may differ in the sort of "maintained hypotheses" that each uses. For example, a common maintained hypothesis in experimental economics is

*The assistance and comments of Bill Bottom, Jon Davis, Nick Dopuch, Tom Fields, Mort Pincus, Chuck Schnitzlein, Bob Tucker, and David Wallin are gratefully acknowledged. Financial support was prcvided by the KPMG Peat Marwick Research Fellowship Program.

that agents' desire for financial rewards dominates other nonfinancial considerations. Behavioral research, on the other hand, may investigate the manner in which psychological factors affect financial considerations. The behavioral research that generates much of the debate between behavioralists and economists tends to be research that could be characterized as being in the early phase of the theory-data feedback loop (it places less reliance on theory to guide data collection).

That research suggests that assumptions made by economic theorists about the decision-making capabilities of agents do not necessarily characterize typical agents. For example, behavioral research has shown that under certain conditions individuals deviate from the economic notion of "rationality" by being prone to representativeness bias, framing effects, preference reversals, and availability bias. The reliability of these findings has been disputed by some economists, who question the validity of the methods used to gather the data.[2] One role experimental economics can play is the investigation of the conditions under which economic incentives, markets, and institutions bring agents' behavior in line with the assumptions of economic models. In addition, the experimental economics approach can enhance development of economic models by identifying settings in which misspecifications about the assumptions of agents affect the predictions of the models, even after controlling for incentives and institutions.

Consistent with the three objectives listed in the first paragraph, this paper attempts to provide a perspective on experimental economics that facilitates a discussion of the advantages and disadvantages of the method in conjunction with other methods in accounting research. Experimental economics has the potential to extend the modeling and empirical feedback process, particularly in accounting and auditing where the institutions found in naturally occurring settings are very complex and difficult to model. Rather than viewing institutions as neutral mutations, experimental economics allows researchers to investigate their roles and assess the relative effects they have on agents' behavior in strategic settings.[3]

In the next section I will provide a brief review of the experimental economics paradigm. This review is followed by an overview of the auditing research that has used the experimental economics paradigm. The fourth section provides a discussion of future research possibilities that link experimental economics and behavioral auditing research. The chapter ends with a summary.

Experimental Economics

This section begins with a presentation of the concept of a microeconomic system. Then there is a description of the general view taken about testing theories using the experimental economics paradigm, which is followed by a discussion of the control features necessary to draw inferences from an economic experiment. The section closes with an example of a hypothetical research project that compares two settings: one where disclosures are mandated to be truthful and one where disclosures do not have to be truthful. The purpose is to integrate the discussion of the experimental economics method into a concrete example.

Experimental economics has developed as a research paradigm primarily to (a) test economic theories, (b) investigate the effects of public policy decisions, and (c) compare the effects of different institutions (see Berg, Coursey, & Dickhaut, 1990; Davis & Swenson, 1988; DeJong, Forsythe, & Uecker, 1985b; Forsythe, 1986; Roth, 1986; Smith, 1982; Smith, Schatzberg, & Waller, 1987; and Wilde, 1980; for reviews). According to Smith (1982), the central concept of experimental economics is a microeconomic system that contains an environment, a trading institution, and subject behavior as its three basic elements (see Figure 1). The environment for a representative agent is the listing of his/her values and costs of economic commodities and a listing of the agents' characteristics such as his/her preferences, knowledge, and resources. The environment of an economic system consists of all agents' characteristics.

The trading institution of a microeconomic system refers to the form and rules governing communications, contract possibilities, the ordering of subjects' moves, and the allocation of economic costs and benefits.[4]

ENVIRONMENT

List of Economic Commodities
List of Agents' Characteristics
Utility Function
Knowledge Endowment
Commodity Endowment

TRADING INSTITUTION

Language Consisting of Messages
Rules for Allocating, Pricing, and Assigning Rights

AGENT BEHAVIOR

Messages Chosen Given the Environment and Trading Institution

Figure 1. The three elements of a microeconomic system

The third element, subject behavior, is the agents' possible selection of messages from the menu, given the existing trading institution and environment. The messages selected by subjects are the empirical observation generated by the experiment.

Experimental methods are used in most realms of scientific research to assess the validity of theoretical predictions under controlled conditions. A formal theory is a systematic mapping of assumptions into theorems. Testing theories is accomplished by contrasting the implications of the theories with observations that allow a partitioning of the data into falsifying and nonfalsifying sets. That is, the theory should have an empirical interpretation that provides evidence that may support an update of beliefs with respect to that theory. Empirical observations, in general, are measured with error. Therefore, observations that are nonfalsifying only implies that the theory is false (lower predictive power) with a lower probability. A set of tests of any theory generally will produce conflicting results. These conflicts can be used to extend or modify the theory. In general theories are not falsified; rather they either fall "out of vogue" or are replaced by theories that have better explanatory power and that are more general.[5]

Early tests of any theory ideally involve a lenient interpretation so as to give the theory its best shot at success (nonfalsification). This should be done primarily because initial tests of a theory are joint tests of the theory itself and the procedures, interpretations, and operationalizations of the test. If the early tests provide support for the theory, more demanding tests can be undertaken to investigate the boundary conditions beyond which the theory may not hold. If the theory regularly "fails" in simple tests, a reexamination of the theory may be useful.[6]

In order to draw inferences from observing messages of subjects, the microeconomic system must incorporate rules governing the distribution of rewards across subjects. Smith (1982) and Wilde (1980) identify four control features (or precepts) required to ensure control over subjects' preferences for experimental commodities. Nonsatiation requires that subjects always prefer receiving more of the reward medium to less. Salience requires a "linkage" between the message choices of the subject and the payoffs received. Dominance requires that the "value" of the rewards received from participating in the experiment are greater than the cost (economic and noneconomic) of acquiring them. Privacy requires that subjects know only their own payoffs. Subjects' risk preferences need to be considered for controlled conditions in situations of uncertainty (see Berg, Daley, Dickhaut, & O'Brien, 1986; Forsythe, 1986; Selto & Cooper, 1990; and Walker, Smith, & Cox, 1989; for a discussion of inducing risk preferences on subjects).

A fifth attribute (beyond the preceding four precepts) that an experiment must have in order to draw inferences is external validity (referred to as *parallelism* by Smith). This issue is discussed in detail by Smith, Schatzberg, and Waller (1987), who argue that experimental markets are "real" and general theories should apply to such settings. External validity is generalizing the model to naturally occurring settings, not an extrapolation of the experimental data.

Although theory testing is prevalent in experimental economics, a large body of work also considers the effects of different institutions. The focus of this work is an examination of the extent to which institutions affect agent behavior and, ultimately, the microeconomy. Institutions can be studied using experiments even though naturally occurring data are unavailable, or because the institutions of interest (possibly proposed in theories or by policy makers) do not yet exist.

As a means of clarifying this discussion, the stages of a hypothetical research project, which can be related to the preceding points, are presented.[7] The process will be divided into three stages: specifying the research question, designing and executing the experiment, and interpreting the results.

Stage 1: Specifying the Research Question

The research question to be addressed is "What effects (if any) will a rule that requires truthful disclosures have on the pricing of an experimental asset?" The motivation for the study is based on theoretical findings that the existence of credible disclosures can significantly affect market outcomes. Akerlof (1970) provides an analysis of market transactions between sellers (who cannot make credible disclosures about the quality of their products) and buyers. Akerlof predicts that only poor-quality products will be exchanged because buyers cannot distinguish qualities. Sellers with high-quality products exit the market because they would rather keep and use their product than sell it for the price of "average products." But as the high-quality products are removed from the market, buyers reduce the price to reflect the lower quality, which in turn forces more sellers out. This process continues until only the lowest-quality products remain, which are the "lemons" traded for lemon prices.

Grossman (1981) analyzed a similar setting, but allowed sellers to credibly communicate their product's quality.[8] With credible communications, Grossman (1981) shows that sellers fully reveal the quality of their products. Sellers with high-quality products would not remain silent (and receive offers consistent with an "average" product) but would identify their product as high quality (buyers believe the disclosure because sellers can't lie) and buyers price it as high quality. In like fashion, sellers with medium-quality products would not remain silent because by identifying the quality of their product they would receive more than being pooled with poor-quality sellers. Therefore, all qualities are communicated except the lowest quality, which is revealed by the silence of the seller.

The intended research compares two "institutions," one where false disclosures are possible and one where they are not. In order to compare the institutions, the setting must be clearly specified. The experiment suggested here (like most), does not follow the theory exactly, but attempts to capture the salient underlying features of the theories.

Stage 2: Designing and Executing the Experiment

Assume a setting with two agent types, a seller and multiple buyers who transact within a single period. The seller has an asset available to sell (with zero reservation value[9]) to the buyers which, if purchased, pays a liquidating dividend of either four dollars or zero dollars to the purchaser. The asset can be one of two types: a high type that pays four dollars with .90 probability and a low type that pays four dollars with .10 probability. During the period,the seller makes a disclosure about the asset type to the buyers who then bid for the asset. The time line depicting the sequence of events is as follows:

1. The seller is endowed with an asset.
2. The seller makes a disclosure to the buyers.
3. The buyers submit bids for the asset and the trade takes place.
4. The asset payoff is determined and cash balances are adjusted.

To generate the pricing predictions, the demand and supply schedules that characterize the setting, shown in Figure 2, are used. The supply schedule (line EFGH) is perfectly inelastic at one unit since there is one seller who has but one asset for sale (with zero reservation value). The demand schedules can be constructed only after making assumptions about the buyers' risk preferences and their knowledge. Let us assume that the buyers are risk-neutral, rational maximizers of expected income. Focusing on the different levels of knowledge, first consider the demand schedule given the assumption that buyers know the asset is a high type. In this case, the demand schedule can be drawn as the combination of the horizontal line (line AEI) and the vertical line (IJKLM).

The intersection of the demand and supply schedules at point E suggests that buyers pay $3.60 for the asset. In this environment, the seller captures all the surplus because buyers compete among themselves and increase bids to the point of making zero profits. If buyers are risk-averse, the demand schedule will fall below the line segment AEI, and if buyers have different risk preferences the demand schedule would be a downward sloping step function. The demand and supply curves are specified so that risk preferences of the agents are very unlikely to make a qualitative difference.

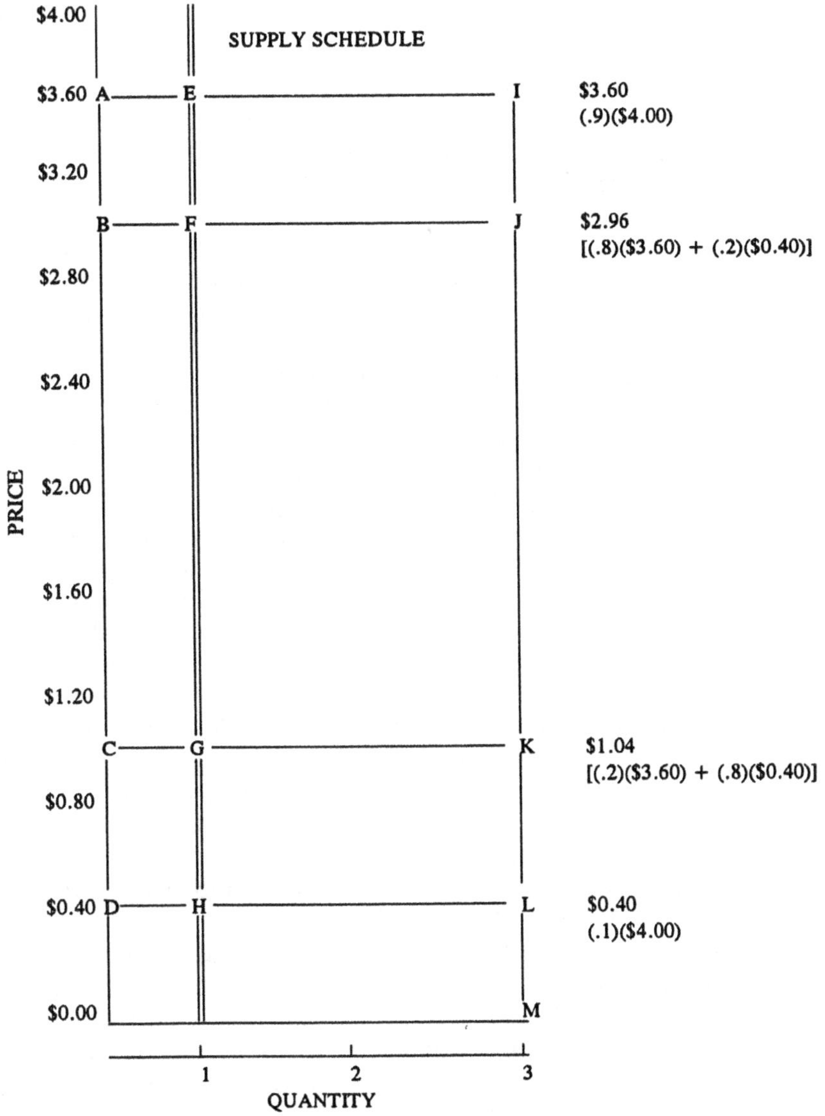

Figure 2. Supply and demand schedules when asset type or investment level is known.

At the other extreme, if buyers know the asset is a low type, the demand schedule is DHLM and the price would be set at \$.40 (point H). Finally, assume that buyers only know the seller's asset is drawn from a distribution of assets that has 20% high assets and 80% low assets. As shown in Figure 2, an asset of unknown type drawn from this distribution has an expected value to buyers of \$1.04 (point G). Recall that the purpose of the experimental test is to compare the effect of an institution requiring all disclosures to be truthful. First to be considered is what would happen in an environment without such a rule by examining the strategies of both the seller and the buyers. The seller wishes to sell the asset for the highest price possible. Figure 2 indicates that will occur when buyers believe the seller holds a high-type asset. But it is not possible for the seller to credibly disclose the high-asset type since the seller can (and will) lie if a low-type asset is held (sellers with low-type assets can costlessly mimic sellers with high-type assets). The predictions are that the seller will disclose the asset as high because that strategy maximizes the price of the asset. Buyers anticipate this disclosure strategy, ignore the disclosure, and price the asset at the expected value of the asset (i.e., \$1.04, point G in Figure 2).[10]

Alternatively, in a setting with only truthful disclosures possible, the seller discloses high when holding a high asset (and buyers price believing the disclosure) and remains silent when holding a low asset. When the seller remains silent buyers price the asset at \$.40 realizing the asset is the low type (otherwise the seller would have disclosed it as high).

At this point the experiment can be designed following as closely as possible the just described setting. The purpose of the experiment is to compare the buyers' pricing and the seller's disclosures for the two disclosure settings.[11] The general procedure is to create a microeconomy populated by economically motivated volunteer subjects. The microeconomic system is established by creating incentives consistent with the theory (see Figure 1).

Assume the researcher decides four subjects would be required—one seller and three buyers.[12] The first requirement to create the microeconomy is to identify the environment. This necessitates the listing of economic commodities and agent characteristics. In this case, the commodity endowment consists of an asset (in the hands of the seller) and cash (in the hands of the buyers). The agents' characteristics are reflected in the specification of the agents' utility functions. The basic requirement is that utility is increasing in cash (agents prefer more money to less). The seller is induced to sell the asset to buyers by paying him/her based on the cash proceeds of the sale. To induce value on the buyers for the asset, the buyer who acquires the asset from the seller is paid by the experimenter based on the actual liquidating dividend value of the asset.[13]

The knowledge endowment is the second of the three variables related to agent characteristics and is a critical feature in this setting. It is assumed that the general nature of the setting (constraints of the disclosure institutions, asset payoffs, probabilities, sequence of moves, etc.) is common knowledge (see Milgrom, 1981b, for a discussion of common knowledge). The only private information is the type of the asset, which is known by the seller but not the buyers. The third variable, commodity endowment, relates to the number of assets the seller is given (assumed to be one) and the amount of cash each buyer has (assumed to be four dollars).

The specification of the institutions requires two sets of rules. The first is the disclosure institution, which specifies the menu from which the seller chooses when disclosing the asset type. This is the variable of interest in this study. The second is the trading institution, which specifies the allocation and pricing of the asset.[14] Assume the second-price sealed bid trading institution is selected. This trading institution allocates the asset to the buyer who submits the highest bid at the price equal to the bid of the second-highest bidder. This trading institution has incentive properties that theoretically induce buyers to bid their reservation value. Theoretically, the second-price sealed bid trading institution is fully demand revealing, which means that buyers can do no better than to bid their value for the asset. The first-price sealed bid institution is not fully demand revealing because agents are predicted to consider the number of buyers who are competing for the asset when submitting bids (see Cox, Roberson, & Smith, 1982).

The final component of the microeconomic system is agent behavior. Agent behavior is observed by placing volunteer subjects in the roles of the players and tracking their messages. Prior to playing their roles, subjects are given instructions that inform them of all aspects of the game.[15] Then subjects are endowed with economic commodities and allowed to undertake the interactions specified by the game (constrained by the environment and institutions). The market described earlier would comprise a single period, but most experiments have multiple periods.[16] At least two markets would be required: one that mandates truthful disclosures and one that does not have this requirement. The predictions for the setting with truthful disclosure are that sellers disclose the high type and buyers price high assets at $3.60 and the low-type ones at $.40. In the setting without truthful disclosures, the seller discloses high (regardless of the type) and buyers bid ignoring the seller's disclosure and price at its expected value.

Stage 3: Interpretation of the Results

In this hypothetical example, no data were generated. Had it been, the analysis would consist of comparing the strategies of the agents across the two disclosure environments. Data generated by experimental markets are not prone to statistical analysis, partly because sample sizes tend to be small. Much of the experimental data to date have been analyzed in an ad hoc fashion using interocular comparisons (e.g., it looks like) or parametric tests because the results and interpretations appeared clear. An example of recent work using sophisticated analysis is Beck, Davis, and Jung (1990). Future research in the area of analysis of experimental data may be very fruitful. If the institutions function as predicted, future work could be considered. An example of work that investigates the efficiency and effectiveness of different institutions designed to generate truthful disclosures is discussed next.

Building on the preceding hypothetical example, Dopuch and King (1990) introduce an institution ("auditing") that is a mechanism with the potential to provide credibility to the seller's disclosures. In addition to the seller and buyers (as discussed earlier), the setting includes an agent who can provide credibility (referred to as a verifier) to the seller's disclosure. The credibility is valued by agents because it has the potential to encourage costly investment by the seller that could make all agents better off.[17] The sequence of steps is as follows:

1. The seller decides whether to hire a verifier at an exogenously specified price.
2. The seller makes the investment choice.
3. The seller is endowed with an asset (probability of the type is based on the investment choice).
4. The seller makes a disclosure to the buyers and the verifier (if hired) makes an investigation choice.
5. The buyers submit bids for the asset and the trade takes place.
6. The asset payoff is determined and cash balances are adjusted.

The costly investment choice increases the probability the asset will be a high type. For example, assume that the costly investment increases the probability the seller receives a high asset from 20 to 80%. Figure 2 showed that the expected value to buyers becomes $2.96 (point J). The increase in economic surplus (rectangle BFGC) is set so as to be greater than the combined cost of the investment and the verifier's investigation. The question investigated in Dopuch and King (1990) is whether moral hazard on the part of the verifier will affect the level of investment by the seller. The results, consistent with the predictions, are that moral hazard on the part of the verifier significantly reduces the frequency of the costly investment.

In the next section some recent auditing studies employing the experimental economics paradigm are reviewed.

Review of Auditing Research Using Experimental Economics

The majority of the work reviewed later has dealt with issues related to the role regulation plays in auditing markets. [Scott (1984) refers to this area as the social role of auditing.] Initial experimental economics studies in this area focus on the demand for and supply of auditing services under varying regulatory conditions.

For purposes here, the existing experimental research in this area is categorized into three basic groups (see Figure 3): (a) research on the relationship between purchasers and producers of services; (b) research on information disclosers and information users; and (c) research considering interactions among information disclosers, users, and "auditors."

Relationship Between Purchasers and Producers of Services

The first experimental market studies bearing on auditing issues focused on the relation between the purchasers and providers of services. This work was pioneered by DeJong, Forsythe, Lundholm, and Uecker (1985); DeJong, Forsythe, and Lundholm (1985); and DeJong, Forsythe, and Uecker (1985a). Common to these studies, three sellers offered to

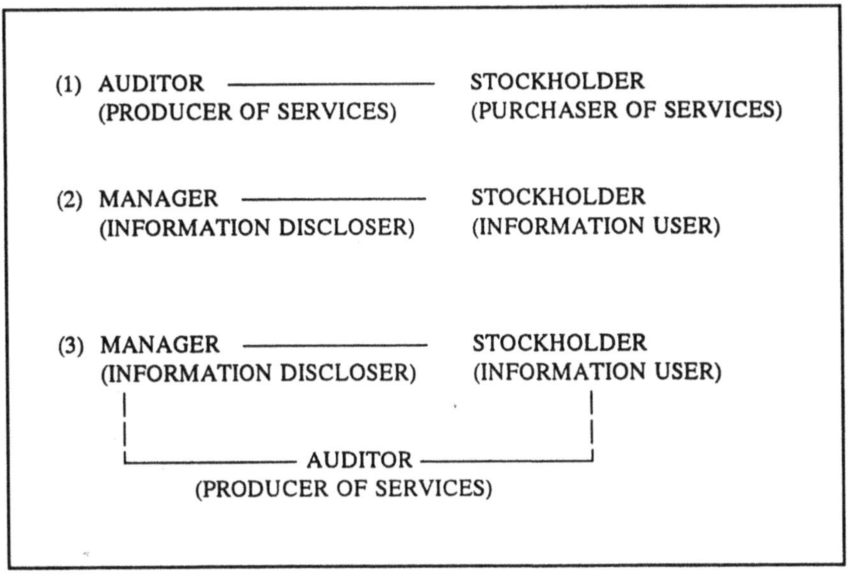

Figure 3. Three basic interactions in auditing experimental economics

sell services of varying quality levels to four buyers, with each seller privately offering to each buyer a promised service level at a specified price. The service commodity provided by the sellers had value to the buyers in that it reduced the probability the buyer would suffer a financial loss. Given the probabilistic nature of the loss, buyers were unable to infer the actual quality level of the service delivered in a specific period, although sellers could form "reputations" for delivering higher-quality services over time. After contracts were made between sellers and buyers, sellers decided which quality level to actually deliver;this could differ from the contracted service level. In some settings, buyers could investigate (at a cost) whether sellers delivered the contracted service quality. When misrepresentations were discovered, penalties were imposed on the sellers. Other settings had liability rules that could be implemented by buyers.

Briefly, it was found that sellers delivered what they contracted for more often than theory predicted when there was neither an investigation option available nor liability rules. In settings with costly investigation, sellers did deliver the contracted quality levels more often, but the improvement in economic efficiency was considerably offset by the cost of the investigations. The main implication of their results is that moral hazard and adverse selection problems may be mitigated by different institutions.

Schatzberg (1990) and Davis (1989) tested predictions specified by DeAngelo (1981) regarding auditor bidding and independence. Schatzberg (1990) investigated the extent of lowballing (bidding below initial period costs) in settings with and without transaction costs (cost of switching auditors and initial engagement startup costs) in a two-period world. He found lowballing in markets with transaction costs, but not in markets without transaction costs. Davis (1989) found (1) that the availability of future quasi-rents did decrease independence and (2) that sunk costs incurred from lowballing (as a response to quasi-rents in competitive markets) further decreased independence.[18] J. Fisher (1987) found that the level of lowballing varied according to the institution used to set auditors' fees. This finding is interesting in that the price-setting institution may be an important decision variable in auditor/client negotiations.

Matsumura and Tucker (1989) first presented a game theory model and then tested it using experimental methods. Their test addressed factors that may influence the level of fraud detection and prevention. They found that an increase in an auditor's liability decreased managerial fraud by increasing the incentives for the auditor to provide a more comprehensive audit.

Relationship Between Disclosers and Users of Information

Although the studies in this area of experimental research do not include an auditor as a participant in the markets, they are germane to auditing since they create environments in which an auditing service might be demanded. Basically these studies address the extent to which possessors of information will disclose this information to others. One of the first studies was by Forsythe, Isaac, and Palfrey (1989) who found that possessors of information did follow the full-disclosure predictions of Grossman (1981) and Milgrom (1981a).

Underlying the full-disclosure prediction is the assumption that buyers of an asset will be skeptical about its quality and assume the worst possible case in the absence of full disclosures. If the sellers anticipate this skepticism, they will fully disclose all information so as not to be thought of as having an asset of the worst quality.

King and Wallin (1991) tested a model of voluntary private information disclosure [based on models by Dye (1985) and Jung and Kwon (1988)]. The model predicts that when receivers of information do not know whether senders actually possess private information, senders will not fully disclose their private information. Potential receivers of information could no longer assume that a failure to disclose fully private information was a sign that the worst state had been attained because there was a positive probability that the sender did not possess any private information. The model predicts that an equilibrium of less-than-full-disclosure will exist in such situations—some private information possessed by the sender that is above the worst case is not released. Although the results from King and Wallin (1991) did not support the specific point predictions of the model, they strongly supported the general proposition that the amount of private information that sellers were willing to disclose decreased with increases in the ex ante probabilities that the sellers did not have private information.

Interactions Among Information Disclosures, Users, and "Auditors"

Kachelmeier (1990) created an experimental setting to investigate the nature of the demand for the attest (or auditing) function when managers and auditors were subject to moral hazard problems. In his setting, "stockholders" contracted with both the manager and the auditors. He investigated whether the managers and auditors could form "reputations" in the multiperiod setting that were not predicted by single-period game theory models.

In his setting, no outcome feedback was provided until the end of the market experiment. His results indicate that the existence of moral hazard on the part of auditors did not cause a significant reduction in overall efficiency because managers selected the costly investment with roughly equal frequency in settings with and without auditor moral hazard. He found that both managerial and auditor shirking were much lower than predicted by single-period models.

M. Fisher (1987) investigated how manipulating the knowledge of materiality levels inherent in an audit report affects market prices, trading volume, and trader profits. She found that public disclosure of the materiality level increased the efficiency of the markets. Although this finding suggests that public disclosures of audit materiality may influence prices, her research setting did not address the issue as to why auditors or managers would be willing to disclose materiality levels.

Dopuch, King, and Wallin (1989) (DKW) investigated the competing demands that sellers and buyers have for disclosure verification. Their results show that sellers were more likely to purchase the services of the auditor than were buyers, and that regardless of who was the purchaser, perfect verification reduced the incidence of moral hazard and adverse selection problems on the part of the seller. They also found the demand for verification was greater when cash payoff feedback was delayed to the buyers. However, the maximum levels of efficiency were not achieved in any of their market settings.

Wallin (1989) investigated managerial demand for auditing in a setting similar to the DKW study. While DKW used a (repeated) single-period model to derive a demand for auditing, Wallin used an unknown-time-horizon approach. With an unknown horizon, the subgame-perfect solution strategy cannot be employed and a cooperative solution becomes a Nash equilibrium.[19] Wallin also investigated the effects of the legal system on cooperation and the demand for auditing.[20]

The level of managerial effort in Wallin when neither auditing nor legal recourse was available was approximately the same as in DKW, despite the change in the time-horizon assumption (other relevant parameters were the same). The presence of auditing caused higher levels of managerial effort and an increase in the "societal benefit" net of audit costs. The presence of a legal system also increased societal benefit net of legal costs. However, contrary to the theoretical assertions, there was a demand for auditing even when the availability of legal recourse led to the highest level of net societal benefit.

Future Research Issues

In this section, I will discuss several issues that may be beneficially addressed by combining advances made in behavioral research and experimental economics.[21] My general belief is that future work may be most fruitfully applied to the area of strategic interactions between competing agents. Auditing is especially sensitive to strategic interactions in that audits are used in determining payoffs for some agents. The anticipation by the auditor of strategic behavior on the part of the manager (and vice versa) is a critical part of their interactions.

Experimental economics studies typically find that agents do not follow the exact normative predictions of game theory.[22] Game theory makes two important assumptions about decision making. First, agents must consider what their strategic counterparts (opponents) are likely to do when contemplating their decisions knowing the opponents are doing the same (and all know this), and second, agents are assumed to be concerned only with their own payoffs.[23] Data from experimental economics research suggest that individuals do not immediately anticipate the strategic choices as game theory models predict.[24] Two possible reasons for the discrepancy will be discussed here: agent skepticism and horizon orientation. Although these reasons are closely interrelated, each will be discussed separately.

The notion of skepticism as envisioned in game theoretic models is that agents always assume other agents are "devious" and select strategies consistent with those devious intentions.[25] For example, if a seller (constrained to tell the truth) disclosed that he/she had a box with five or more apples, buyers are predicted to assume that five apples were in the box. Alternatively, if the seller remained silent, buyers are predicted to assume the box held zero apples (the lowest quantity possible). Experimental evidence suggests agents are not as skeptical as the models predict. It may be that individuals expect others to be "honest" or "fair." This may be due to (a) cultural conditioning, (b) the fact that in some cases individuals are just not able to "put themselves in the shoes of others" and anticipate the opponents' strategies,[26] or (c) the existence of "reputations" as an inherent good.

A second aspect of strategic behavior is horizon orientation. Game theory models assume that finitely repeated single-period games are solved by backward induction. This technique requires that agents first anticipate what will happen in the final period of the game. They then consider what will happen in the second-to-last period, which is solved in the same way the last period was solved since the second-to-last period cannot affect the last period's solution (which was previously determined). Using this process, the same solution unravels back to the first period of the game.

Experimental evidence suggests that agents, in the process of formulating their own strategies, place more weight on evidence of their opponents' previous strategies (backward looking) than on the anticipated strategies in the final periods (forward looking/unraveling).[27] It is only near the end of the game that agents seem to be affected by the shadow of the end. In some cases, agents using backward-looking orientation suffer financial losses to forward-looking opponents who defect from previous strategies.[28]

Auditing is a process that can be sensitive to horizon orientation. The long contract horizons (implicit or explicit) between auditors and clients make it possible for clients to develop a reputation that could be cashed in during bad times. Because the frequency of client failure is typically so low, the normal skeptical attitude may be subject to decay. Future work investigating the effects of horizon orientation could provide insights in modeling the propensity for agents to defect.

Future collaborative research between behavioral auditing research and experimental economics could investigate the types of institutions that help reduce the efficiency losses from strategies that are not predicted to be optimal. For example, previous research has considered cost-free decision aids. The implementation and evolution of costly institutions and decision aids that enhance efficiency and allow stable and predictable patterns of behavior may be useful for accounting and auditor researchers.

Summary

Accounting research using experimental methods has evolved over the years, in part by importing and customizing innovative research methods and techniques of analysis developed in the disciplines of economics and psychology. The objective of this paper was first to present an overview of current research in auditing using experimental economics techniques and then discuss future research possibilities. The basic message from experimental economics is that economic institutions matter. Auditing and accounting are basically economic institutions that play an important role in the operation of capital markets and the design of corporate organizations. Research that enhances the understanding of these roles should be encouraged.

In hindsight, it may be that behavioral and economic research has been slow in integrating each others' developments and findings. Part of the reason for this may be that the exchange between the research groups has not promoted a movement toward "middle ground." For example, some economists have been accused (perhaps correctly) of hiding behind the rigor of their models, and when confronted with contradictory evidence, challenging the behavioral researcher to produce a "better model." Requiring psychologists to do fundamental economic theory development is not an efficient use of resources. Experimental economics has the potential to employ the strengths of both economics and behavioral research. The issues in accounting and auditing allow collaborative ventures with behaviorists modeling the information processing and judgment aspects of agents and experimental economists modeling institutions and competitive forces. Such ventures could provide benefits for both research paradigms.

Endnotes

1. The term "institution" is used in two ways in this paper. The first way, as defined by Smith (1982), is as a language for participants in a microeconomy (see Figure 1). The second way is consistent with Langlois (1986, p. 247), who defined institutions as "rules or sets of rules that constrain or govern organized patterns of behavior." Smith's definition can be used in a broad sense also, but it has been primarily used to refer to trading institutions. In order to differentiate the two meanings, when referring to Smith's definition, *trading* institution will be used.

2. Some of the charges leveled against this research are that (a) the settings were "one shot" trials and were without economic institutions, (b) the tasks (usually hypothetical in nature) did not have actual monetary consequences, and (c) they omitted the disciplining aspects of markets. See Cox and Isaac (1986), Grether (1980), and Thaler (1986) for a discussion of this debate.

3. As a result, experimental economics complements emerging theoretical work in accounting and economics, which more fully incorporates the interactions between decision makers, institutions, and markets. Traditional assumptions used in economic models have included cognitively unbounded economic agents who are rational expected utility maximizers, firms as production functions, markets without transaction costs, and economic systems without economic institutions (see Coase, 1988). Economists are currently engaged in developing models that (a) relax the extreme "rationality assumptions" (Arrow, 1986); (b) view firms as economic institutions (Williamson, 1985); and (c) investigate the purpose and efficiency of markets (Smith, 1982).

4. More precisely, the trading institution specifies the final commodity allocations, cost imputation rules, payment rules, and sequencing of communication between subjects (Smith, 1989).

5. See Lakatos (1978) and Smith (1989) for a discussion of theory evolution.

6. The issue of generalizing experimental results is debated actively. Most discussions focus on whether results "confirmed" in the laboratory carry over to the real world. A second controversy relates to whether theories "falsified" in the laboratory could be appropriate in the richer setting of the real world. It is clear, though, that if a theory is examined first in a rich setting and it does

not perform well, it is difficult to determine whether the theory or the procedures of the test are at fault.

7. This example is, in part, based on research by Dopuch, King, and Wallin (1989) and Dopuch and King (1990).

8. Credible disclosures require the seller to always disclosure truthfully. This could be due to an antifraud rule associated with disclosures. Theoretically, such a rule can be operationalized by the existence of some agency, which can impose such a "large" penalty for lying that the rule is never violated. Vague disclosures (e.g., remaining silent) are not violations of the antifraud rule. King and Wallin (1990) test the relative abilities of two different mechanisms to provide credibility—an ex ante antifraud rule and ex post verification.

9. Grossman (1981) implicitly assumes sellers have "low" reservation values relative to buyers. Increasing the seller's residual value in the asset could have important implications, but this is not considered here.

10. The setting is a single-period one. Reputations for "honesty" would be possible (but not predicted) in a multiperiod setting with a known finite end.

11. The specification of the buyers' preferences would be critical if the test involved point predictions of the asset price. However, the intended test is to compare the relative effects of the two disclosure institutions. Several methods of dealing with risk preferences have been used in previous experimental economics, and this is an issue of emerging importance. For purposes of this example, the assumption of risk neutrality is maintained.

12. The number of buyers is set so as to have sufficient competition for them to bid their reservation price. It is costly to have numerous buyers both in the money paid to them and the possibility that boredom may set in. If buyers purchase assets only infrequently, bids could lose saliency. Previous research suggests three buyers should satisfy these constraints.

13. Average payments to participants in experimental economic markets typically range from \$8.00 to \$20.00 per hour.

14. One thrust of experimental economics has been the consideration of trading institutions. Frequently, models do not specify how prices are set. Researchers using experimental methods must explicitly consider the pricing mechanism when designing experiments.

15. The operation of the experiment can be conducted by hand (having messages sent on paper notes and keeping track of cash balances on paper) or by computer. Computers offer the advantage of reducing paper work, which allows subjects to focus on their decisions and not on record keeping. See Williams (1980), who compared "oral" and computer markets. Computer markets allow agents more privacy in real time markets (e.g., double auctions) because agents cannot see one another during the trading. This is an important advantage when investigating the role information plays in market equilibria.

16. In general, experimental markets consist of multiple periods. This allows subjects to become familiar with the procedures and adjust to the strategies of other agents (and in the process, converge to an equilibrium).

17. The truthful disclosure institution specified in the hypothetical example did not have any value given the assumptions about risk preferences. The seller would have the same expected return in the two disclosure settings.

18. The two studies differ on a number of dimensions. Davis (1989) uses a five-period world, whereas Schatzberg (1990) used two periods. Schatzberg restricted the bids in the second period so that the auditor could not suffer a loss over the two periods, whereas Davis did not. These two studies make a very interesting comparison of the different way two researchers (both trained in experimental economics) working independently on a similar topic, could develop quite different settings to test the same basic theory.

19. A Nash equilibrium requires that agents select strategies such that no party wishes to unilaterally defect.

20. See Axelrod (1984) for a discussion of cooperation in prisoners' dilemma games.

21. See Libby (1989) for a discussion of the potential interactions between behavioral decision theory research and experimental economics in the area of human information processing and Smith, Schatzberg, and Waller (1987) for a discussion of possible auditing research topics that focus on economic models.

22. Behavioral research has generally used a decision theoretic orientation, whereas most experimental economics research has employed a game theoretic orientation. The game theoretic approach used in experimental economics has been noncooperative

rather than cooperative game theory. Noncooperative game theory differs fundamentally from cooperative in that binding commitments are impossible in non-cooperative theory. See Camerer (1988) for a discussion of behavioral game theory.

23. This issue will not be discussed here, but bargaining research using experimental methods has shown that the knowledge of payoffs to others does matter in strategy selection.

24. In many cases, strategies do converge (with replication) to the theoretical predictions in simple settings.

25. No one is hurt by this devious posture since all agents know about it and adjust their strategies accordingly. Financial harm to particular agents could result if they are not sufficiently skeptical. A lack of skepticism could be beneficial in some cases, if it is used to maintain a tacit arrangement for "cooperation."

26. Possible explanations for (b) are that the Nash Equilibrium solution concept may not be descriptively accurate or the context of the interactions [state variables or noise (see Bendor, 1987)] makes it difficult for agents to decipher the strategy choices of their opponents. Future research could investigate how agents update their beliefs after receiving sample evidence in situations where the evidence is subject to manipulations (Shibano, 1990).

27. This is not to say end-game effects are not important. They are, but the history of actions on the part of other agents may be more important until the very last few periods of the game. See Camerer and Weigelt (1988) for results of an experimental test investigating end-game strategies.

28. In some cases, backward-looking strategies Pareto dominate Nash strategies (e.g., the tit-for-tat strategy in prisoners' dilemma game).

6
Predictive Bankruptcy Judgments by Auditors: A Probabilistic Approach

William N. Dilla, Richard G. File, Ira Solomon, and Lawrence A. Tomassini*

Auditing is a human evaluation process to establish the adherence to certain norms, resulting in an opinion.
(Schandl, 1978, pp. 2–3)

Audits play a key role in market-based economies. Financial statement audits, in particular, facilitate the corporate form of business in which those who own assets (i.e., stockholders) are separated from those who employ them (i.e., corporate management). Because of their importance in the U.S. economic system, the effectiveness of audits has become the focus of considerable attention by regulators and researchers. Any consideration of such effectiveness, however, must start with a shared understanding of the nature and purpose of auditing.

Among several possible perspectives, Schandl's definition (above) is most useful for present purposes. This definition highlights that auditing is an evaluation process, the quality of which is dependent upon the effectiveness of auditors which, in turn, depends on the quality of judgments (and decisions) made during the audit process. Many such judgments are generic to most audits, including determining what and how much evidence is needed, as well as when such evidence is to be obtained. Also, the need to judge the extent of conformance of financial statement information with the relevant criteria (e.g., generally accepted accounting principles) is a generic task among audits.

Within the last 15 years, the auditing scholarly and practice communities have gained appreciation for the relevance and importance of psychological research. Indeed, many auditing studies published since the mid-1970s have employed psychological research methods and tested

*We are grateful to Don Kleinmuntz and the participants in the Accounting Colloquium at The Ohio State University for comments on earlier drafts of this manuscript.

psychological theories. Such studies typically have focused on the interrelated issues of how auditors make judgments and decisions and how well they make them. This component of the audit literature has become sufficiently sophisticated to contribute to the psychological literature (e.g., Anderson & Wright, 1988; Ashton & Ashton, 1990; Tomassini, Solomon, Romney, & Krogstad, 1982). Therefore, a two-way street has evolved between the academic disciplines of auditing and psychology.

One of the more important judgments that auditors make regards the continued viability of the audited company as a business enterprise. Auditors refer to this as the *going concern judgment*, and this judgment must be incorporated into every financial statement audit. Because a going concern assumption is fundamental to interpreting published financial statements, current auditing standards stipulate that auditors must formulate a judgment about whether the audited company will be able to continue in existence or will experience bankruptcy (AICPA, 1988). Additionally, recent increases in the business failure rate in certain industries (e.g., savings and loan) make it incumbent upon today's auditors to pay even more attention than in the past to the possibility of bankruptcy.

This chapter describes an empirical study of auditors' predictive bankruptcy judgments. The first purpose of the study is to assess the quality of those judgments and determine the dependency of that quality on the specific prediction made (bankruptcy or non-bankruptcy) and the level of analysis (aggregate or individual). Formulating bankruptcy judgments is viewed herein from the Bayesian perspective of decision making under uncertainty. Importantly, this perspective suggests the importance of certain criteria (conformance with the probability axioms and probability calibration) for appraising judgment quality. The second purpose of this study is to ascertain the empirical association between these probabilistic quality measures and the accuracy measures ("hit rates") typically employed in the accounting bankruptcy prediction literature.

The remainder of this chapter is presented in five sections. The next section describes the audit judgment/decision setting and reviews prior relevant research, thereby providing the background for the present paper. Section three describes the method of our study, and section four reports the experimental results, which are then discussed in section five. Concluding remarks complete the chapter.

Background

Audit researchers (e.g., Kraft, 1968) recognized over two decades ago that the audit may be characterized from a Bayesian perspective. Focusing at the level of an individual account, the auditor adopting this perspective formulates a proposition (hypothesis), implicitly or explicitly quantifies his/her prior (perhaps subjective) knowledge about the proposition in the form of a prior probability distribution, and then conducts a preposterior analysis to determine how much additional (typically objective sample) information must be gathered before a decision can be made. Following this determination, the auditor gathers such information and combines it via Bayes' rule with the prior information to form a posterior probability distribution. A choice then is made, based upon the prior and objective sample information, by constructing a credible interval on the posterior distribution or by minimizing costs, as represented by some loss function.

Characterizing the audit process in this fashion has produced many valuable research insights. Much of the research providing these insights has focused on assessment of probability distributions formally representing the auditor's prior knowledge. Such prior knowledge either involved the reliability of the information (control) system producing the financial statements or the financial statement accounts themselves.

Prior Studies of Auditor Probability Assessment

Corless (1972) reported the first of three studies investigating whether auditors could specify information from which prior probability distributions could be constructed for information system error rates. Auditors in the Corless study employed either the fractiles or fixed-interval method to formalize their prior beliefs. Corless reported that the auditors were able to specify prior probability distributions, but that there was considerable variability among the specified distributions, both within auditors (between different probability elicitation methods) and between auditors (using the same elicitation method).

Felix (1976) focused on auditors' ability to employ a probability elicitation method in which the assessor must think of his/her subjective beliefs as equivalent to a hypothetical prior sample. When used in the context of evaluating an information system, the equivalent-prior-sample (EPS) method requires specification of two values, r' and n', so that the prior knowledge is equivalent to having observed a sample of r' occurrences in a sample of size n'. Felix reasoned that, because of auditors' familiarity with sampling, this elicitation method would provide a natural frame for formalizing auditors' subjective knowledge. In spite of the intuitive appeal of this method, auditors had difficulty using it. Felix found it especially troublesome to coordinate the degree of subjective confidence felt by the auditor and the n' to be specified. Crosby (1981) also relied on the intuitive appeal of the EPS method to motivate his study. Using essentially the same experimental task as Felix (1976), Crosby reported that his auditors had greater facility with the method and that the specified prior probability distributions did not differ significantly (in mean or variance) as a consequence of using the EPS method or another method.

Solomon, Krogstad, Romney, and Tomassini (1982) reported an early study of account balance probability elicitation. In particular, they found that practicing auditors could use the fractiles elicitation method to specify prior probability distributions. Importantly, such distributions conformed with conventional audit wisdom about the likelihood of overstatements of asset accounts; they also exhibited certain desirable characteristics, including being more (less) diffuse (representing greater [lesser] uncertainty) when the auditee's control system was relatively poor (good). In another account balance study, Solomon, Tomassini, Romney, and Krogstad (1984) investigated auditors' ability to employ the EPS method. However, the problems identified by Felix (1976) in the information system appraisal context appeared in Solomon et al. (1984) and were even more pronounced in the account balance context.

Whether in the context of appraising information system reliability or verifying recorded account balances, prior research has focused on auditors' ability to use alternative elicitation methods. Further, these studies generally have employed rather simplistic criteria for appraising the viability of such methods (e.g., convergent validity—the extent to which assessed distributions differed by elicitation method, and whether conventional wisdom about characteristics of such distributions was reflected therein). In settings such as auditing, however, notions of goodness more closely tied to performance are especially important (see Davis & Solomon, 1989). For probability judgments, conformance with the probability axioms (sometimes called "normative goodness") and calibration have been suggested as performance-based criteria. Well-calibrated judgments conform with outcomes in the following sense—across all events for which an evaluator states that there is an X% chance of occurrence X% of the time the event occurs (see Lichtenstein, Fischhoff, & Phillips, 1982). When the assessed probability of occurrence exceeds that actually observed, the assessor is said to be *overconfident*, while the assessor is said to be *underconfident* when the latter exceeds the former.

In general, probability calibration is important because a set of miscalibrated probabilities violates the axioms (i.e., a "dutch book" can be made against the assessor). In auditing, probability miscalibration has been linked to compromising the effectiveness or efficiency of the audit by predisposing the auditor to conclude incorrectly that a financial statement account balance is (is not) in conformance with specified criteria (see Beck, Solomon, & Tomassini, 1985).

Probability calibration has been investigated in only three published studies of auditor judgments. Tomassini et al. (1982) examined the calibration of auditors' account balance prior probability distributions. The most striking result was an inconsistency with the typical finding when probability calibration is measured: in the aggregate, there was no evidence of overconfidence. Indeed, while in a relative sense, the judgments were well-calibrated, there was a tendency toward underconfidence. This research was extended in two related studies. In Solomon (1982), various group approaches to probability assessment were investigated. Consistently, it was reported that there was no evidence of overconfidence. Last, Solomon, Ariyo, and Tomassini (1985) reported that when auditors made probability assessments for general information (almanac) questions, overconfidence resulted. Consequently, it was suggested that contextual features of probability assessment tasks are quite important and that the auditors' underconfidence probably was due to some aspect of the audit context or the account balance assessment task.

Prior Studies of Bankruptcy Prediction

Bankruptcy prediction studies have a rich heritage in the accounting literature. This line of research includes statistically oriented studies, using methods such as multiple discriminant analysis and (more recently) probit and logit analysis, as well as behaviorally oriented studies in which humans make predictive bankruptcy judgments (see File, 1981; Zavgren, 1983; and Zmijewski, 1984, for reviews). Irrespective of whether a statistical model or human judge makes the prediction, however, two elements typically are common to such studies. First, accounting cues, usually a set of financial ratios, provide the basis upon which the bankruptcy prediction is made. Second, the criterion for evaluating prediction goodness is some form of hit rate (however, see Lau, 1987, for an exception).

Several variations of the hit-rate criterion have been used, but most commonly, researchers have focused on minimizing the complement of the hit rate (i.e., the false-negative and/or false-positive error rates).[1] When the focus is on predicting bankruptcy (as opposed to continued viability), a false-negative error occurs when a bankrupt firm is predicted to be nonbankrupt, while a false positive error occurs when a nonbankrupt firm is predicted to be bankrupt. In addition, because the costs of false-negative errors (e.g., investing in a firm that goes bankrupt) generally are thought to exceed the costs of false-positive errors (e.g., the opportunity cost of failing to invest in a firm that is successful), researchers often have weighted the two error rates differentially.

Research Questions

Based on the preceding discussion, we address four research questions in this paper. First, in the *aggregate* (across individuals), how well calibrated are auditors' predictive bankruptcy judgments? Recall that prior research has reported that, for the task of account balance estimation, auditors' probability distributions exhibited a tendency toward underconfidence. This question attempts to extend this finding to the context of bankruptcy prediction. One noteworthy difference between the two tasks is that, for the account balance task, continuous probability assessments were obtained; in the bankruptcy prediction task (described later), discrete probabilities were elicited.

Second, to what extent does auditor calibration depend on the specific prediction made (bankrupt or not bankrupt)? If a significant dependency were to exist, global analysis of aggregate auditor calibration in bankruptcy prediction would not be particularly useful.

Third, how well calibrated are individual auditors in predictive bankruptcy judgments? In the typical study, calibration is measured in the aggregate (across individuals) because there are usually too few observations from any individual subject to obtain stable estimates. To the extent that there are no substantial calibration differences among subjects, aggregation would seem to be acceptable. However, if large differences exist, the practice of aggregating subjects' judgments could mask the calibration deficiencies that the researcher is attempting to identify and could alter an interpretation of the solutions to auditor miscalibration.

Fourth, how highly correlated is individual-level calibration with more traditional accuracy (hit-rate) measures of prediction performance? If high correlation exists, our confidence in the results of other studies of predictive bankruptcy judgments would be reinforced. However, if these performance criteria are not highly correlated, we might wish to reconsider conclusions based on hit rates in the predictive bankruptcy judgment literature.

Method

This section describes the details of the method employed to address our research questions.

Participants

Participants in the study were 36 practicing auditors who were employed in three major public accounting firm offices in two large Southwestern cities. The auditors were selected on the basis of availability and willingness to participate. They had a mean experience level of approximately three years and had other demographic characteristics typical of such personnel in these firms (a university education of at least the undergraduate level, etc.).

Task

The auditors' task was to make 40 predictive bankruptcy judgments, one for each of 40 real companies that were hypothetically treated as audit clients. Specifically, the auditors were told to assess the probability that each company would go bankrupt within three years. We provided the auditors with the following information to facilitate these judgments: (a) six key financial ratios for each company in each of the two previous years; (b) a base rate for bankruptcy, communicated by informing the auditors that the sample of companies was randomly drawn from a population that had an actual bankruptcy rate of 30% during the subsequent three-year period; and (c) a statement identifying the companies as industrial firms listed on either the New York or American Stock Exchanges and whose financial statements (and the derivative ratios) had been subjected to an audit.

The Financial Ratios

The financial ratios provided for each company were: (a) the current ratio (total current assets divided by total current liabilities), (b) the return on assets ratio (net income divided by total assets), (c) the cash-to-total-assets ratio, (d) the current-assets-to-total-assets ratio, (e) the current-assets-to-sales ratio, and (f) the debt-to-equity ratio (total liabilities divided by total owners' equity). We selected these particular ratios because of minimal redundancy and their relatively high predictive ability (see Kennedy, 1975; Libby, 1975).

Sample Client Firms

From an initial set of 53 firms that went bankrupt during the period 1973–77, according to the *Wall Street Journal Index*, 12 were randomly selected to represent the 30% bankrupt cases among the company set evaluated in the experiment. Each of these companies was listed in *Moody's Industrial Index* and had financial statement information available for at least three years preceding bankruptcy.

In addition to these 12 bankrupt firm cases, a sample of 28 firms that did not go bankrupt within the subsequent three years were randomly selected from *Moody's*. The total of 40 firms (12 bankrupt and 28 nonbankrupt) was combined and randomly sequenced in the experiment.

Procedures

Each auditor was given an envelope containing the research materials. These materials included a set of instructions, the financial ratios for each of the 40 companies (on 40 separate pages), and a brief demographic questionnaire. For each company, the auditors were instructed to express the probability of bankruptcy as a percentage between 0 and 100. They had one hour to complete the task.

Performance Measures

To address our research questions, we computed performance measures for the aggregation of all 36 auditors and for each individual auditor. In particular, at the aggregate level, we computed the relationship between assessed probabilities (expected frequencies) and actual frequencies of the bankruptcy/nonbankruptcy predictions and expressed that relationship by plotting half-range calibration curves. For such curves, responses on the diagonal suggest perfect calibration, and those significantly below (above) the diagonal suggest overconfidence (underconfidence) in the aggregate sample. We used the following procedures to develop the calibration curves:

1. We classified all predictions as either "bankrupt" (> .5) or "nonbankrupt" (< .5). Responses of exactly .5 (96 out of 1440 total responses) were omitted as being nonpredictions.
2. We scaled all half-range data between .51 and 1.0. Therefore, all responses below .5 were transformed as (1.0 − *p*) to express the probability in terms of the maintained prediction.
3. We divided the half range into five deciles: .51–.60, .61–.70, .71–.80, .81–.90, and .91–1.00. Then we used the mean of the assessed probability for each of these ranges as the predicted frequency for purposes of comparison with actual frequencies of bankruptcy/nonbankruptcy. Also, we performed a sensitivity analysis on this division into deciles (categories), but our results were qualitatively unaffected.
4. For each curve, we plotted five data points, each point representing the correspondence between the mean probability assessed (predicted frequency) in each decile category and the actual frequency of the predicted event (bankruptcy or nonbankruptcy).

At the individual level, we computed (a) a half-range five decile-based calibration score relating to the appropriateness of auditor confidence (expressed uncertainty level) and (b) a correct classification/accuracy percentage (hit-rate score). Following Lichtenstein and Fischhoff (1977), we used the first three steps from plotting aggregate calibration curves and the following computation to determine the principal calibration scores (see Oskamp, 1962):[2]

$$\text{calibration} = \frac{1}{N}\sum_{t=1}^{T} n_t |p_t - c_t|, \tag{1}$$

where N is the total number of probability assessments (40 in this study), n_t is the number of times the probability response p_t was used, c_t is the percentage of correct predictions (hit rate) for each category (decile), and T is the total number of response categories used (5 in this study). A perfectly calibrated auditor would have a score of 0.00.

As a secondary descriptive performance measure, we computed an over/underconfidence score for each auditor, as follows:

$$\text{overconfidence/underconfidence} = \frac{1}{N}\sum_{t=1}^{T} n_t(p_t - c_t). \qquad (2)$$

Overconfidence (underconfidence) is indicated by a significantly positive (negative) score. The over/underconfidence measure allows an assessment both of the magnitude and direction of any miscalibrated probability assessment, limited, however, by the potential offsetting of positive and negative deviations. The principal calibration score has the opposite traits. Note that both of these performance measures depend on a relationship between the mean probabilities assessed and the percentage of correct classifications (hit rate).

Results

Aggregate Calibration (Research Question 1)

We plot the half-range aggregate auditor calibration curve in Figure 1.

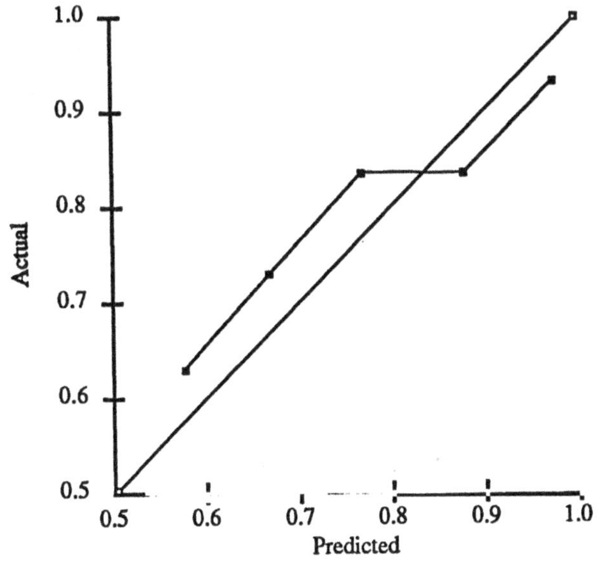

Figure 1. Half-range: all predictions.

This figure indicates a slight tendency toward underconfidence among the auditors, driven primarily by assessments of the less extreme probabilities (i.e., .50–.75 in the half-range probability scale). However, using a chi-square test, this tendency is not significantly different from proper calibration (chi-square = 5.137; df = 4; p > .25).

Calibration Dependency on Type of Prediction (Research Question 2)

We plot another half-range calibration curve in Figure 2. This curve is a decomposition of the curve in Figure 1 and is based on the type of prediction (bankrupt or nonbankrupt) made by the auditors. This plot shows that nonbankruptcy predictions exhibit a strong underconfidence tendency, while the bankruptcy predictions, although more mixed, exhibit a tendency toward overconfidence. Using the chi-square test, the miscalibration for nonbankruptcy predictions is highly significant (chi-square = 20.049; df = 4; $p < .001$), while the miscalibration for bankruptcy predictions is moderately significant (chi-square = 8.454; $p < .10$).

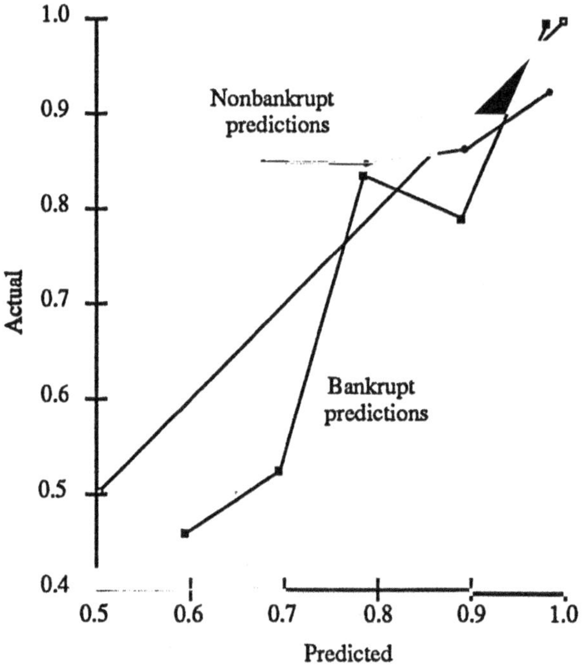

Figure 2. Half–range bankrupt and nonbankrupt predictions.

Table 1 Panel A.
Statistics for Individual Auditors

A	B	C	D	E
Subject number	Calibration (Oskamp)	Percentage correct	Mean response	Over (under) confidence
1	0.172	0.684	0.645	−0.039
2	0.089	0.769	0.719	−0.050
3	0.089	0.775	0.774	−0.001
4	0.253	0.889	0.636	−0.253
5	0.184	0.775	0.694	−0.082
6	0.184	0.621	0.655	0.035
7	0.151	0.833	0.788	−0.046
8	0.158	0.833	0.675	−0.158
9	0.066	0.718	0.712	−0.006
10	0.094	0.719	0.684	−0.034
11	0.087	0.744	0.715	−0.028
12	0.090	0.725	0.680	−0.045
13	0.170	0.703	0.860	0.157
14	0.143	0.639	0.635	−0.004
15	0.096	0.838	0.742	−0.096
16	0.092	0.757	0.841	0.084
17	0.181	0.769	0.719	−0.050
18	0.154	0.794	0.757	−0.037
19	0.112	0.711	0.696	−0.015
20	0.123	0.850	0.740	−0.110
21	0.112	0.757	0.780	0.023
22	0.173	0.784	0.941	0.157
23	0.192	0.656	0.823	0.167
24	0.081	0.790	0.727	−0.062
25	0.114	0.800	0.723	−0.078
26	0.102	0.774	0.734	−0.040
27	0.111	0.800	0.689	−0.111
28	0.166	0.775	0.609	−0.166
29	0.159	0.725	0.721	−0.005
30	0.134	0.750	0.657	−0.093
31	0.141	0.790	0.822	0.033
32	0.177	0.825	0.648	−0.177
33	0.080	0.811	0.810	−0.001
34	0.218	0.775	0.760	−0.015
35	0.120	0.800	0.738	−0.063
36	0.098	0.703	0.801	0.098

Table 1 Panel B
Descriptive statistics for auditors

	Calibration (Oskamp)	Percentage correct	Mean response	Over (under) confidence
Mean	0.135	0.763	0.732	−0.031
Std. deviation	0.044	0.059	0.072	0.091
Median	0.128	0.775	0.722	−0.038

Table 1 Panel C
Calibrations scores and confidence scores

Calibration scores	Number	Over (under) calibration scores	Number
< 0.075	1	< −0.09	8
0.075 to 0.124	17	−0.9 to −0.031	12
0.125 to 0.199	16	−0.03 to 0.03	9
≥ 0.20	2	0.031 to 0.09	3
		> 0.09	4

Individual Calibration (Research Question 3)

In Table 1, we list the key descriptive statistics for each individual auditor and some supplementary summary statistics. According to the table, the miscalibration (column B) of our auditors ranges from Oskamp scores of .0664 to .2528, with a mean of .1352. The bulk of our auditors was miscalibrated in the 8 to 20% range. The strength of this principal calibration measure is that it considers both overestimates and underestimates and does not permit them to offset each other. However, the direction of the miscalibration is not identified.

The over/underconfidence scores indicate the direction of miscalibration, while adding noise due to offsetting of overestimates and underestimates in some instances. As Table 1 Panel A indicates, these secondary measure scores (column E) range from −.1777 to +.1672. As Table 1 Panel C shows, the bulk of these auditors are underconfident. Using a 95% confidence interval around a score of 0.00, which ranges from −0.030 to 0.030, we determine that 20 auditors (55.6%) are underconfident, 9 auditors (25%) are well-calibrated, and only 7 auditors (19.4%) are overconfident.[3] Further, the mean of the 36 scores is

$-.0309$, representing (on average) significant underconfidence for the sample ($t = -2.038$; df = 35; $p < .05$).

Comparison of Individual Performance Criteria (Research Question 4)

Hit rates for each auditor also are listed in Table 1 Panel A (column C). The association between these hit rates and the individual calibration scores (.04) is not significantly different from 0.00 at conventional levels.

As a secondary descriptive analysis, we correlated hit rates with the auditors' over/underconfidence scores. The association was $-.61$ ($p < .0001$). We also ran the analysis in decomposed form, separating those with positive and negative over/underconfidence scores. The association was significant for auditors with negative over/underconfidence scores ($r = -.65$; $p < .001$), but not for those with positive scores ($r = .12$; $p > .70$).

Discussion

Aggregate Calibration (Research Question 1)

In this study, we viewed client bankruptcy predictions by experienced auditors as probabilistic judgments. The first research question involved a description of the appropriateness of confidence expressed by these auditors while making such judgments. Our results indicate that, in the aggregate, the auditors exhibited a slight tendency toward underconfidence, particularly for middle-range probabilities. However, the aggregate auditors were statistically indistinguishable from proper calibration. This aggregate performance is contrary to most of the probability calibration literature (Lichtenstein et al. 1982), but it is similar to the tendency reported in the Tomassini et al. (1982) study of experienced auditors in an account balance task.

Calibration Dependency on Type of Prediction (Research Question 2)

Our second result is a calibration asymmetry, based on prediction type. That is, to the extent that our results generalize, predictions of bankruptcy tend to be overconfident, and predictions of nonbankruptcy tend to be underconfident. This finding is important for at least three reasons. First, it highlights the danger in making inferences solely from global calibration results. That is, more meaningful insights may be gained by decomposing responses into subtypes before performing calibration analyses.

Second, and related, this finding suggests that ad hoc adjustments made to recalibrate probability assessments in a bankruptcy task do not

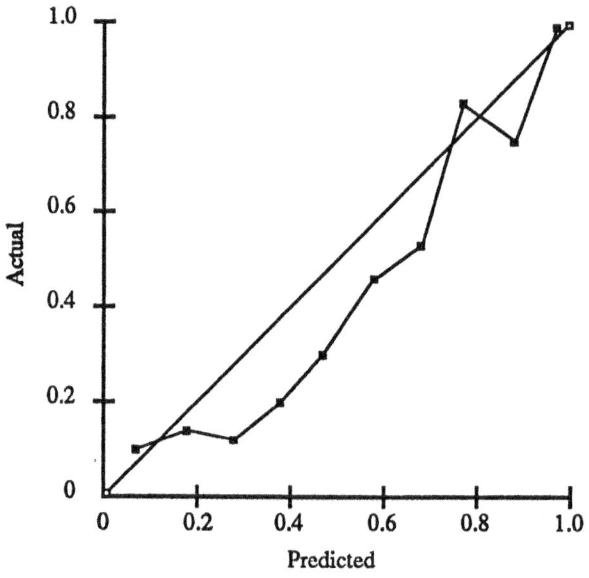

Figure 3. Full range: all predictions.

depend on the type of prediction made. In this instance, the full-range probability assessment scale may be useful to analyze for predictive bankruptcy judgments. As shown in Figure 3, for both the bankruptcy predictions (i.e., $p > .50$), which reflect overconfidence, and the nonbankruptcy predictions ($p < .50$), which reflect underconfidence, the probabilities assessed (on average) exceed the actual frequency of bankruptcy. Thus, recalibration efforts can be consistently directed toward making negative (downward) adjustments to the assessed probabilities of bankruptcy, regardless of the ultimate prediction made.

Third, our results are consistent with the possibility that auditors confound beliefs and preferences in their expressed probability assessments. A false-negative error in this context (i.e., the risk of predicting nonbankruptcy when the firm is going bankrupt) is probably perceived to be more costly than a false-positive error (i.e., the risk of predicting bankruptcy when the firm is not going bankrupt) (see, for example, File, 1981). If auditors confound their probability assessments by "adjusting" for the excess cost of false-negative errors, they will tend to overstate consistently the probability of bankruptcy, irrespective of whether they believe bankruptcy or nonbankruptcy is more likely. Also, this possibility is consistent with one of the speculative interpretations of the auditor calibration results in Tomassini et al. (1982).

Individual Calibration (Research Question 3)

Many studies in the probability calibration literature present only aggregate results. One of the unique contributions of the present study is our investigation of how much variation in individual probability calibration exists within a set of experienced auditors. Our results show that noticeable variation does exist. While the aggregate calibration results suggest that auditors' judgments are quite well-calibrated, few if any of the individuals could be considered well calibrated, according to the Oskamp measure. Further, consistent with Tomassini et al. (1982), the bulk of individual auditor miscalibration appears to be in the direction of underconfidence.

These results suggest that further research is needed to explain individual differences in probability assessment skill among what might seem to be a very homogeneous pool of professionals. Also, these results suggests that researchers should be careful not to overgeneralize from the typical calibration study data, which totally relies on aggregate-level analysis.

Comparison of Individual Performance Criteria (Research Question 4)

The final result of our analysis shows the lack of association between calibration and hit-rate performance scores. However, underconfident auditors appear different; the greater their hit rates, the more underconfident they tend to be. The reason for this tendency can be gleaned from the lack of association between hit rates and mean probabilities assessed (in this case, $r = .06$).

Recall that the over/underconfidence score, discussed earlier, is affected by both the mean probability assessed and the percentage correct (hit rate). Therefore, a negative association between the over/underconfidence score and hit rate could be due to either (a) a decrease in mean probability assessments as hit rates increase or (b) an insensitivity of probabilities assigned to hit rates (i.e., mean probabilities remain constant as hit rates increase). The result here reveals that the underconfident auditors in particular do not realize their improvement in accuracy (mean probability assessments are insensitive to improvements in hit rates).

Typical bankruptcy judgment studies in accounting (e.g., Libby, 1975) use hit rates as the criterion variable. However, our results suggest that using a probabilistic judgment framework as an alternative to traditional bankruptcy prediction evaluations may yield significant empirical, as well as theoretical, differences. In addition, bankruptcy prediction studies that rely on one or the other measure may paint an incomplete performance picture.

Concluding Remarks

Finally, we offer some comments on future research opportunities. The present study, combined with Tomassini et al. (1982), suggests that auditor judgments may provide fertile ground for psychological investigation of probability assessment. While we have observed that experienced professional auditors tend to be slightly underconfident, we lack good theory and a clear psychological interpretation of these tendencies. Further research is needed to provide such insights, both to aid the improvement of auditing practice and to enrich the growing psychological literatures on expertise and decision making under uncertainty. In conducting such research, we must consider that the experimental task needs to produce sufficient data for individual-level calibration analysis.

With respect to the criteria used to study judgments, such as those made by practicing auditors, our results suggest that researchers should be careful to build multiple criteria into evaluations of probabilistic judgment quality. Further, we should consider extending research studies that have relied entirely on hit rates, using a probabilistic judgment framework such as the one we employed. Also, psychologists may be able to enhance our understanding of results such as those presented here and in Tomassini et al. (1982) by addressing why experts are insensitive to how much they know. Overall, a partnership between psychology and auditing scholars is needed. While psychologists are most familiar with the constructs and assumptions (e.g., loss ratios) embedded in calibration measures, auditing scholars understand the salient institutional features of audit decision settings and how these features translate into particular loss ratios. Both the accounting and psychology academic communities have much to gain from continuing to pave our two-way street.

Endnotes

1. In the bankruptcy prediction literature, such errors usually are referred to as Type I or Type II error rates, respectively. However, technically, those terms refer to hypothesis testing tasks, rather than the evaluation task in bankruptcy prediction.

2. The Oskamp score assumes a linear loss function. We also used a score based on a quadratic loss function, but our results were not qualitatively affected. The two forms of calibration scores were correlated .90 with one another.

3. Arguably, the 9 auditors who are labeled as well-calibrated have non-trivial Oskamp calibration scores (range = .0664 to .2182 and mean = .1185), which are only slightly below those of the other auditors. Apparently, the over/under-confidence scores approximating 0.00 are due to the aforementioned cancellation of positive and negative errors.

7
A Test of the Relationship Between Task Structure and Decision Aids Type in Auditing

Mohammad J. Abdolmohammadi*

Introduction

A classification of audit tasks by level of complexity is advocated in the literature for automation of structured tasks and for developing decision support systems (DSS) and knowledge-based expert systems (KES) to aid the auditor in semistructured and unstructured tasks (Abdolmohammadi, 1987; Messier & Hansen, 1984). This literature is based on the works of organizational scientists and decision aid theorists who suggested a correlation between task structure and decision aids. For example, Simon (1960) suggested a model of decision process whereby the process is viewed as three distinctive phases—intelligence, design, and choice—which have implications for the level of programmability of the specific decision context. Based on the work by Simon (1960), Keen and Scott-Morton (1978) suggested a model of task structure and decision aids with a positive correlation between task structure and decision aid types.

In auditing, studies of audit structure of the firm (Cushing & Loebbecke, 1986) and audit task structure within each firm (Abdolmohammadi, 1990) have been done indicating that auditing

*This chapter is based on part of a data base developed under a grant from the Peat, Marwick, Mitchell Foundation's Research Opportunities in Auditing Program. The views expressed are those of the author and do not necessarily reflect the views of the Foundation. The author gratefully acknowledges the participation of the 49 partners and managers from three international accounting firms who spent some three hours on the task instrument in this study. The author is also grateful to the participants at the audit symposium at State University of New York at Albany and the Critical Perspectives in Auditing Conference in New York City, particularly Bill Messier and Ira Solomon for their helpful comments.

researchers and practitioners should give more formal consideration to the structure question. What is not clear is whether in fact audit task structure and decision aids are correlated. Specifically, does the model of task structure and decision aids apply to the audit setting? The objective of this chapter is to investigate this issue by providing evidence on task structure judgments and decision aid choices of highly experienced auditors.

Organization of this chapter is as follows: the next section provides the Simon model of the decision process, task structure, and decision aids, followed by a section on the research design. The analysis of the data is presented in the third section, followed by the final section, a summary and conclusions.

A Model of the Decision Process, Task Structure, and Decision Aids

According to the Simon (1960) model, any decision process encompasses three iterative phases: intelligence, design, and choice. Carlson (1983) summarizes these phases as presented in Figure 1. The intelligence phase relates to the definition of the problem under consideration and collection of data relating to the problem. At the design phase, the decision maker would generate alternative courses of action and collect further data if necessary to support each alternative. Analysis of the alternatives and the selection and explanation of the best alternative are done in the choice phase.

For example, suppose an auditor is evaluating the adequacy of a client's allowance for doubtful accounts. The auditor might take the following approach: (a) prepare (or have the client prepare) a list of credit customers with their corresponding account balances (intelligence phase); (b) classify customers into different risk groups by preparing an aging schedule (design phase) and send confirmation letters accordingly; and (c) choose a given percentage of the balances of each risk group as allowance for doubtful accounts (choice phase).

In some tasks, the problem can be well-defined at the intelligence phase and alternative solutions are very limited at the design phase, leaving very little judgment needed to make a final choice at the choice phase. These tasks are considered to be "programmable" (Simon, 1960). Keen and Scott-Morton (1978) called these tasks "structured." There are other tasks where the problem is ill defined at the intelligence phase and the alternative solutions may be numerous at the design phase, requiring the decision maker to use considerable judgment and insight to choose an alternative at the choice phase. These tasks are called "nonprogrammable" (Simon, 1960) or "unstructured" (Keen & Scott-Morton, 1978).

INTELLIGENCE
Gather data
Identify objectives
Diagnose problem
Validate data
Structure problem

DESIGN
Gather data
Manipulate data
Quantify objectives
Generate alternatives
Assign tasks or values to alternatives

CHOICE
Generate statistics on alternatives
Simulate results of alternatives
Explain alternatives
Explain choice

Figure 1. Decision-making phases.**

Somewhere between the programmable-nonprogrammable or structured-unstructured continuum lie other tasks. These tasks may be called "semiprogrammable" or "semistructured" (Keen & Scott-Morton, 1978). While the problem in these tasks could be reasonably defined at the intelligence phase, alternative solutions may be limited and specified at the design phase, leaving some judgment to the decision maker in choosing among the alternatives at the choice phase of the decision process. The top panel of Figure 2 summarizes the phases of the decision process along the structured-unstructured continuum.

An implication of this model in auditing is that the less structured the task, the more the need for decision support. At the structured task level, automation of the process is feasible. A major portion of these types of tasks is in fact already automated in large accounting firms (see Grease, 1984, for Peat, Marwick, Mitchell's experience).

Semistructured tasks, on the other hand, require more than automation. The decision maker can use data and models to assist him/her in choosing between alternatives. DSSs have been proposed in the literature to provide this assistance (Abdolmohammadi, 1987). For example, internal control evaluations are considered by auditors to be a semistructured task (Abdolmohammadi & Wright, 1986). This is because, while the problem of internal control evaluation is reasonably

**From Carlson (1983, p. 137), adapted with permission.

	Task Structure		
Decision Phase	Structured	Semistructured	Unstructured
Intelligence:			
Problem is	Well defined	Reasonably defined	Ill defined
Alternatives:			
Are:	A few	Limited	Numerous
Choice:			
Requires	No judgment	Some judgment	Judgment and insight
Decision support:	Automation	Decision support system	Knowledge-based expert system

Figure 2. Relationships between task structure and decision aids***

defined at the intelligence phase, and alternative decisions are limited (e.g., strong, mediocre, or weak) at the design phase, the auditor needs to use some judgment to choose among alternatives at the choice phase. Bailey, Duke, Gerlach, Ko, Meservy, and Whinston (1985) have developed a decision support system called TICOM to assist auditors in designing, evaluating, and analyzing internal control systems.

In the unstructured task category, consider the task of evaluating the controls in an advanced electronic data processing system. This task may be unique for each audit and present many possible alternatives, leaving the choice phase of the decision process in need of much judgment and insight on the part of the advanced EDP auditor. Thus, the decision aids necessary in this task would require the consideration of the decision rules used by a specialist auditor (e.g., computer audit specialist). KESs have been proposed in the literature for these tasks domains (see Abdolmohammadi, 1987). The EDP-Xpert system developed and tested by Hansen and Messier (1986) is an example of such a system. The lower panel of Figure 2 summarizes the implication discussed earlier.

The discussion just presented suggests a positive correlation between task structure and decision aid types. Thus, the model in Figure 2 suggests that audit tasks classified by level of structure would present

***From Abdolmohammadi (1987),adapted with permission.

opportunities for automation of structured tasks, DSS development for semistructured tasks, and KES development for unstructured tasks.

The suggested relationship between task structure and decision aids has not been tested in auditing. Accounting firms are increasingly incorporating structured audit approaches (standardized tools and techniques) and a top-down approach to the design and execution of an audit engagement (Cushing and Loebbecke, 1984, 1986). Furthermore, based on audit models and models borrowed from other fields, academic and professional authors (e.g., Bedard, Gray, & Mock, 1984; Elliott & Kielich, 1985; Hansen & Messier, 1986; Keith, 1985) have proposed certain audit tasks for decision aids development. It is the objective of this study to provide initial evidence of empirical relationship between task structure and decision aid types in auditing.

Hypotheses

The expectation from the Keen and Scott-Morton (1978) model depicted in Figure 2 is that there would be a significant positive correlation between task structure and decision aid type. Thus the central hypothesis is stated as:

> H_1 There will be a positive correlation between task structure and decision aid type.

However, the Simon model of the decision process has a characteristic that may be particularly relevant to auditing. The model classifies tasks as "programmable" or "nonprogrammable." Although decision aid theorists have taken these terms essentially as equivalents to "structured" and "unstructured" tasks, such equivalence may not apply to auditing. In auditing, a task may be viewed as structured and yet may be subject to strictly human processing (i.e., not programmable). For example, consider the task of inventory observation. The auditor may view this task not as a simple structured task but as a task that lends itself to strictly human processing rather than automation.

The implication is that the model depicted in Figure 2 applies only to tasks that are viewed by auditors as subjects of some sort of decision aid development. Thus, the tasks that are viewed by a majority of subjects to be performed only by strictly human processing should be deleted from the analysis. Therefore:

> $H_{1.1}$ Positive correlation between task structure and decision aid type is limited to a subset of audit tasks where strictly human processing is not considered to be the most appropriate by a majority of auditors.

Research Design

To study the relationship between task structure and decision aid, there was first a need for a complete inventory of audit tasks. The task inventory developed by Abdolmohammadi (1990) was used to collect data on task structure judgments and decision aid choices of auditors. This section provides information on subjects, an overview of the project, and the questionnaire scale.

Subjects

Since only high ranked auditors are involved with decision aids choices within accounting firms, participation of managers and partners was requested for the study. Based on a pilot study with three partners and two managers, it was estimated that the time requirement would be three hours to respond to all questions in the study, including the decision aids choices and task structure judgments. Accordingly, the time requirement was a major commitment on the part of the subjects. To enhance participation of these subjects, the author made sure that the quality of the task instrument was at the highest-possible level. The author also secured support of a very high ranking partner in each of seven offices of three Big-Eight accounting firms in Boston, Chicago, and New York. These coordinating partners were then sent a packet containing 11 copies of the task instrument. They were instructed to keep one copy for their own perusal and distribute the remaining 10 copies among partners and managers in their offices or offices in the regions under their authority. In addition, they were requested to collect the completed questionnaires and send them back to the author.

Six offices of three accounting firms cooperated, but having completed only one questionnaire, the seventh office decided not to continue because the time spent on the first questionnaire was five hours. This was significantly greater than the time commitment the author had requested. Of the 61 questionnaires distributed, 49 were completed and returned, making the response rate over 80%. Of the 49 respondents, 14 were partners, 33 were managers, and one was a supervising senior. One respondent did not fill out the demographic questionnaire. The mean experience level of the subjects was 10.01 years (standard deviation, 5.56). The average time spent on the task instrument was 160.93 minutes (with 45.21 standard deviation). Consequently, the time spent was, on the average, less than the three hours requested; this did not differ significantly from firm to firm.

Overview of the Project

For a project of this magnitude, it was important that each of the terms used be as clearly understood as possible. Accordingly, based on

Abdolmohammadi and Wright (1986) and the results of the pilot study, a three-page overview was attached to the task instrument. In this overview, the Simon (1960) model was presented in a nontechnical way and related terminology was briefly defined with a nonauditing example following.

The Questionnaire

The task complexity questionnaire had an instruction page, which provided a list of the six main parts of the audit process from orientation to financial statement reporting. The six parts were adapted from Felix and Kinney (1982) and *KPMG Peat Marwick Manual-US* (1987). These parts are (a) orientation, (b) preliminary evaluation of internal controls, (c) compliance tests of controls, (d) substantive tests, (e) forming opinion, and (f) financial statement reporting.[1]

The instruction sheet asked that the subjects evaluate each of 332 tasks for level of complexity and mark their responses in the appropriate space that appeared opposite each task. The method chosen for eliciting this information was a 1 - 9 Likert scale where 1 - 3 was assigned to structured tasks, 4 - 6 was assigned to semistructured tasks, and 7 - 9 was assigned to unstructured tasks. This partitioned scale was chosen based on Abdolmohammadi and Wright's (1986) experience. In that study, although a 1 - 27 scale was attempted (three point spreads for each point in a 1 - 9 scale), the responses actually were close to a 1 - 9 scale; subjects in that study showed a tendency toward the middle of each three-point spread.

The subjects were then requested to choose the appropriate decision aids for each of the 332 audit tasks. The choices were among four alternatives: automation (AU), decision support systems (DSS), knowledge-based expert systems (KES), and strictly human processing (HP). The definitions of these terms were provided to the subjects in the overview part of the questionnaire. Although there is no universal definition of decision aids in the present literature, for the purpose of this study, the following definitions were adopted (and provided to the participants in the instructions to the questionnaire) from Abdolmohammadi (1987):

> *Complete automation:* Some audit tasks such as footing, recalculation, and cross-checking may be done completely by a computer based on some predetermined formula. This is referred to as complete automation.
>
> *Decision support systems* (DSS): A DSS is an interactive computer-based software that assists decision makers in making decisions. DSSs use certain models (e.g., statistical or

mathematical models in analytical review procedures) and data to make inferences for the use of the decision maker.

Knowledge-based expert systems (KES): A KES is interactive computer-based software that assists decision makers in using expert(s) decision rules to make their decisions. To create a KES, the decision rules of the expert(s) must be elicited and expressed in terms of a number of "If-Then rules." To employ a KES, the decision maker provides answers to questions posed by the system. The KES then presents a recommendation to the decision maker. The decision maker has the option of accepting or rejecting the recommendation developed by the KES.

Strictly human processing: Some audit tasks may not be suitable for automation, DSS, or KES. These tasks require strictly human processing. It should be noted that all decision aids have a human processing component to them.

The numerical equivalents assigned to these choices were 1 for AU, 2 for DSS, 3 for KES, and 4 for HP. Accordingly, although the decision aid choices were categorical, correlation analysis can be done on numerical equivalents to study the relationship between task structure (1 - 9 scale) and decision aid types (1 - 4 scale).

The Results

To analyze the data for H_1, first a summary of all data is presented. Thus if the predicted positive relationship exists between task structure and decision aid types, significant correlations must be found for a majority of audit tasks. To formally study this, the nonparametric Spearman rank correlation between task structure and decision aid type was calculated for all tasks. Since by nature a large portion of tasks in auditing are performed strictly by human processing, the next analysis will be focused on tasks for which over half of the subjects chose some form of decision aid rather than strictly human processing. This was done to test for $H_{1.1}$.

To prepare a summary of all data, task structure responses were classified as follows: (a) 0.00 - 2.50, structured; (b) 2.51 - 3.50, structured/semi-structured; (c) 3.51 - 5.50, semi-structured; (d) 5.51 - 6.50, semi-structured/unstructured; and (e) 6.51 - 9.00, unstructured.

This classification schema was adopted because the differences between (a), (c), and (e) were generally statistically significant (depending on the standard deviation for each task) between the audit

Table 1. Task structure, experience, and decision aids*

	Task Structure					
Audit part	0.00–2.50	2.51–3.50	3.51–5.51	5.51–6.50	6.51–9.00	Total
Orientation:						
No. of tasks	1	6	14	14	10	45
Mean Dec. Aid	3.48	3.28	3.56	3.64	3.86	3.61
Internal Control:						
No. of tasks	1	4	34	2		41
Mean Dec. Aid	3.86	3.61	3.64	3.81		3.65
Compliance Tasks:						
No. of tasks	1	4	24	5		34
Mean Dec. Aid	3.82	3.12	3.58	3.79		3.57
Substantive Tests:						
General and ARP:						
No. of tasks			5	2		7
Mean Dec. Aid			2.95	3.70		3.16
Cycles:						
No. of tasks	77	37	49	1		164
Mean Dec. Aid	3.40	3.45	3.68	3.63		3.50
Forming Opinion:						
No. of tasks			2	14	7	23
Mean Dec. Aid			3.92	3.88	3.94	3.90
Financial Statement Reporting:						
No. of tasks			7	10	1	18
Mean Dec. Aid			3.80	3.84	3.94	3.83

*No. = number; Dec. Aid = decision aid assigned to the task;
ARP = analytical review procedure.

tasks, but category (b) was not significantly different from either category (a) or category (c). Similarly, category (d) was not found to be significantly different from either category (c) or category (e). Therefore, categories (b) and (d) were viewed to be borderlines between other clear classes of audit tasks. Table 1 shows the number of tasks in each part of the audit that were classified into the five categories of structure. Table 1 also presents the means of the subject responses on decision aid choices.

As Table 1 shows, the means of decision aids selected for tasks are 3.00 or above for all parts of the audit with the exception of tasks in the general and analytical review procedures (ARP) in the substantive tests part of the audit. The mean response for this part is 2.95. The data indicate a heavy tendency toward human processing choice (coded as 4) for the subjects regardless of the structure classification of the tasks. Consequently, Table 1 does not lend support for H_1; an overall positive relationship between task structure and decision aid type is not evident from the data.

Looking at the detailed data, the author observed that only in some tasks in the risk assessment area (EDP auditing issues and analytical review procedures), did the participants indicate the use of decision support and expert systems.

Interestingly enough, it is in these areas that there already are some decision support and expert systems developed both by academicians and practitioners. Similarly, in only a few tasks in the test of details of transaction cycles, is there evidence in support of automation. Again the profession is already using software such as spreadsheet programs to completely automate such tasks (e.g., footing, recomputation). To further analyze the data for H_1, and provide analysis for $H_{1.1}$, Table 2 was prepared. The first column in Table 2 presents data on all tasks. Out of the 332 tasks in the study, only 43 (13%) show significant Spearman rank correlation between task structure and choices of decision aids at the .05 level. Thus a majority of tasks (87%) show no significant correlation.

Therefore, contrary to H_1, only a small percentage (13%) of the tasks showed significant correlation between structure of the tasks and decision aid type. Furthermore, an observation from the correlation data was that of the 43 significant correlations, there were four significant negative correlations. These negative correlations related to tasks that were

Table 2. Proportion of tasks with significant correlation between task structure and decision aid choices

Measure	All tasks	Non-HP tasks
Significant correlation tasks	43	16
Total tasks	332	35
Ratio	13%	48%

viewed to be relatively structured but they lend themselves to only strictly human processing. All four tasks related to vouching in the substantive tests of transactions and balances part of the audit. For example, the task of "vouching of purchases and other disbursements from purchases journal to supporting documents including quantities, prices and other relevant data" was given a mean structure classification of 1.94, indicating the task is a structured task. However, 47 of the 49 subjects viewed the task as subject to strictly human processing, resulting in a −.378 Spearman correlation (significant at the .05 level) with the task structure. There were many negative correlations (albeit not statistically significant) in many tasks. This represents an interesting characteristic of the audit process: the task may be classified as structured but not programmable.

The second column in Table 2 presents the total number of tasks that were viewed by over half of the subjects as applicable for some form of decision aid rather than strictly human processing. Out of the 35 such tasks, 16 (48%) showed significant positive correlation between the task structure and choices of decision aids. None of the tasks indicated negative correlation. An example of these tasks is the "assessment of the profitability of the entity relative to its industry," which was viewed as a border-line structured-semistructured task (mean structure classification = 3.45). While only five subjects chose automation to be appropriate for this task, 25 subjects chose decision support system and 8 chose expert system for it. The remaining 11 subjects viewed the task as subject to strictly human processing. The Spearman correlation coefficient of .348 was significant at the .05 level. Therefore the data indicate that consistent with $H_{1.1}$, for the tasks that are not chosen for strictly human processing by the majority of subjects, positive relationship between task structure and applicable decision aids is supported.

Summary and Conclusion

This study provided evidence on the relationship between task structure and perceived applicable decision aids for a comprehensive listing of audit tasks. It tested the Simon (1960) model of programmable to nonprogrammable tasks, finding support from the audit data collected in the study. However, the general model of positive relationship between task structure and decision aids suggested by Keen and Scott-Morton (1978) was not fully supported by the data. Only in the case of tasks for which the majority of subjects chose some form of decision aid (as opposed to strictly human processing) was the Keen and Scott-Morton model supported.

The results have implications for the research and development efforts in decision aids in auditing. For example, the Keen and Scott-Morton model suggests that once tasks are classified by level of structure, decision aids can be developed accordingly: automation for structured tasks, decision support systems for semistructured tasks, and knowledge-based expert systems for unstructured tasks. However, the results in this study indicate that decision aids research and development must go beyond this model to identify the tasks that are programmable regardless of their degree of structure. Only in the case of 13% of the 332 tasks was the Keen and Scott-Morton model supported and there were four significant negative correlations there. This changed to 48% for the subset of tasks that over half the subjects viewed as appropriate for some form of decision aid development. Furthermore, there were no negative correlations in this subset.

The perceptions of the subjects who indicated that a majority of tasks are applicable for strictly human processing rather than some form of decision aid is interesting. However, while in some tasks, even structured (e.g., consideration of whether canceled checks cleared the bank within a reasonable time of recording), strictly human processing makes sense; in many other tasks decision aids have theoretical appeal. Since the responses are from very experienced auditors, it may be that these individuals are reflecting the old way of performing audit tasks rather than the potential of new technology. Collection of data on certain factors such as training in and/or experience with the use of new technology may shed light on this issue.

Comparative studies of different fields of inquiry to investigate the issue of relationship between task structure and decision aid types are also of interest. Do the results reported in this study hold for other fields such as law, psychological counseling, etc. where professional judgment is the backbone of the field? If so, does this mean that the models developed by organizational theorists and decision aid researchers are not robust enough to be applied to judgmental fields? What are the opportunities for developing field-specific models of task structure and decision aids? Who is really qualified to provide choices of task structure and decision aids within each of these fields? Does a high level of experience provide the quality needed for such choices or should context-specific specialties be considered for studies of this sort? Future research is needed to consider these questions.

Endnote

1. Discussion of the details of these phases is beyond the scope of this paper. The interested reader is referred to Felix and Kinney (1982) and Abdolmohammadi (1990).

References

Abbott, A. (1988). *The system of professions: An essay on the division of expert labor*. Chicago: The University of Chicago Press.

Abdel-Khalik, R., & El-Sheshai, K. M. (1980). Information choice and utilization in an experiment on default prediction. *Journal of Accounting Research, 18*, 325–342.

Abdolmohammadi, M. J. (1987). Decision support and expert systems in auditing: A review and research directions. *Accounting and Business Research, 77*, 173–185.

Abdolmohammadi, M. J. (1990). *A taxonomy of audit task complexity and experience requirement in auditing*. Unpublished manuscript, Bentley College, Waltham, MA.

Abdolmohammadi, M. J., & Wright, A. (1986). A classification of audit task complexity for developing decision aids. *Proceedings of the 18th National Meeting of Decision Sciences Institute*, Honolulu.

Abdolmohammadi, M. J., & Wright, A. (1987). An examination of the effects of experience and task complexity on audit judgments. *The Accounting Review, 62*, 1–13.

Akerlof, G. (1970). The market for 'lemons': Quality uncertainty and the market mechanism. *Quarterly Journal of Economics, 84*, 488–500.

American Institute of Certified Public Accountants. (1988). The auditor's consideration of an entity's ability to continue as a going concern. *Statement on Auditing Standards No. 59*. New York: Author.

Anderson, D., & Stokes, D. (1988). *Product differentiation in audit firms*. Unpublished manuscript, The University of Queensland, St. Lucia, Queensland, Australia.

Anderson, M. (1985). Some evidence on the effect of verbalization on process: A methodological note. *Journal of Accounting Research, 23*, 843–852.

Anderson, U., & Marchant, G. (1989). The auditor's assessment of the competence and integrity of auditee personnel. *Auditing: A Journal of Theory and Practice, 8*, 1–16.

Anderson, U., & Wright, W. (1988). Expertise and the explanation effect. *Organizational Behavior and Human Decision Processes, 42*, 250–269.

Arrow, K. (1982). Risk perception in psychology and economics. *Economic Inquiry, 20*, 1–9.

Arrow, K. (1986). Rationality of self and others in an economic system. *The Journal of Business, 59*, S385–399.

Asare, S. K. (1990). *The auditor's going concern opinion decision: Interaction of task variables and the sequential processing of evidence*. Unpublished manuscript, Fisher School of Accounting, University of Florida, Gainesville.

Ashton, A., & Ashton, R. H. (1988). Sequential belief revision in auditing. *The Accounting Review, 63*, 623–641.

Ashton, A., & Ashton, R. H. (1990). Evidence-responsiveness in professional judgment: Effects of positive versus negative evidence and presentation mode, *Organizational Behavior and Human Decision Processes, 46*(3), 1–19.

Ashton, R. H. (1982). Human information processing in accounting, (Studies in Accounting Research No. 17). Sarasota, FL: American Accounting Association.

Ashton, R. H., & Ashton, A. H. (1990). Evidence-responsiveness in professional judgment: Effects of positive versus negative evidence and presentation mode. *Organizational Behavior and Human Decision Processes, 46*, 1-9.

Ashton, R. H., & Willingham, J. J. (1988, May). *Using and evaluating audit decision aids*. Paper presented at the Touche Ross/University of Kansas Auditing Symposium, Lawrence.

Awasthi, V., & Pratt, J. (1988). *The effects of perceptual differentiation and monetary incentives on problem solving performance in accounting settings*. Unpublished manuscript.

Axelrod, R. (1984). *The evolution of cooperation*. New York: Basic Books, Inc.

Bailey, A. D., Duke, G. L., Gerlach, J., Ko, C., Meservy R. D., & Whinston, A. B. (1985). TICOM and the analysis of internal controls. *The Accounting Review, 60*, 186–201.

Baiman, S., & Lewis, B. L. (1989). An experiment testing the effectiveness of screening employment contracts. *Journal of Accounting Research, 27*, 1–20.

Bamber, E. M. (1983). Expert judgment in the audit team: A source reliability approach. *Journal of Accounting Research, 21*, 396–412.

Bamber, E. M. (1987). *The effect of perceived expertise on auditors' review judgments*. Unpublished manuscript, Fisher School of Accounting, University of Florida, Gainesville.

Bamber, E. M. (1988). *An organizational perspective on the audit methodologies issue*. Unpublished manuscript, Fisher School of Accounting, University of Florida, Gainesville.

Bamber, E. M., & Bylinski, J. H. (1982). The audit team and the audit review process: An organizational approach. *Journal of Accounting Literature, 1*, 33-58.

Bamber, E. M., & Bylinski, J. H. (1987). The effects of the planning memorandum, time pressure and individual audit characteristics on audit managers' review time and judgments. *Contemporary Accounting Research, 4*, 127–163.

Bamber, E. M., & Snowball, D. (1988). An experimental study of the effects of audit structure in uncertain task environments. *The Accounting Review*, *63*, 490–504.

Bamber, E. M., Snowball, D., & Tubbs, R M. (1989). Audit structure and its relation to role conflict and role ambiguity: An empirical investigation. *The Accounting Review*, *64*, 285–299.

Beck, P. J., Davis, J., & Jung, W. (1990). *The economics of taxpayer reporting under uncertainty: Experimental evidence*. Unpublished manuscript, University of Illinois, Champaign.

Beck, P. J., Solomon, I., & Tomassini, L. (1985). Subjective prior probability distributions and audit risk. *Journal of Accounting Research*, *23*, 37–56.

Bedard, J. (1989). Expertise in auditing: Myth or reality. *Accounting, Organizations and Society*, *14*, 113–132.

Bedard, J., & Biggs, S. (in press). Pattern recognition, hypothesis generation and auditor performance in analytical tasks. *The Accounting Review*.

Bedard, J., Gray, G. L., & Mock, T. J. (1984). Decision support systems and auditing. *Advances in Accounting*, *1*, 239–266.

Bendor, J. (1987). In good times and bad: Reciprocity in an uncertain world. *American Journal of Political Science*, *31*, 531–558.

Berg, J., Coursey, D., & Dickhaut, J. (in press). Experimental methods in accounting: A discussion of recurring issues. *Contemporary Accounting Research*.

Berg, J., Daley, L., Dickhaut, J., & O'Brien, J. (1986). Controlling preferences for units of experimental exchange. *Quarterly Journal of Economics*, *101*, 281–306.

Bernard, V. (1990). Capital markets research in accounting during the 1980s: A critical review. In T. J. Frecka (Ed.), *The state of accounting research as we enter the 1990s*, Champaign: University of Illinois.

Berton, L. (1989, May 24). Ernst & Young must marry two styles. *The Wall Street Journal*, p. B6.

Berton, L. (1989, July 7). Andersen, Price Waterhouse are in formal talks; Deloitte Haskins and Touche Ross agree to merge, *The Wall Street Journal*, p. A3.

Biggs, S. F. (1984). Financial analysts' information search in the assessment of corporate earning power. *Accounting, Organizations, and Society*, *9*, 313–324.

Biggs, S. F., Mock, T. J., & Watkins, P. R. (1988). Auditor's use of analytical review in audit program design. *The Accounting Review*, *63*, 148–161.

Blocher, E., & Willingham, J. J. (1985). *Analytical review: A guide to evaluating financial statements*. (New York: McGraw-Hill & Co.).

Bonner, S. (1990). Experience effects in auditing: The role of task-specific knowledge. *The Accounting Review*, *65*, 72–92.

Bonner, S., & Lewis, B. (1991). Determinants of auditor expertise. *Journal of Accounting Research*, *28*, S1–28.

Bonner, S. E., & Butler, S. A. (1989). *Auditor's performance when using attention-directing analytical procedures*. Unpublished manuscript, University of Oklahoma, Norman.

Boritz, J. E. (1986). The effect of research method on audit planning and review judgments. *Journal of Accounting Research*, *24*, 335–348.

Bouwman, M. J., Frishkoff, P. A., & Frishkoff, P. (1987). How do financial analysts make decisions? A process model of the investment screening decision. *Accounting, Organizations, and Society*, *12*, 1–29.

Brown, C. E., & Solomon, I. (1987). Effects of outcome information on evaluations of managerial decisions. *The Accounting Review*, *62*, 564–577.

Brown, S. H. (1981). Why Lasser Found Touche Ross Taxing. *Fortune*, *103*, 10, pp. 103–107.

Butt, J. L. (1988). Frequency judgments in an auditing-related task. *Journal of Accounting Research*, *26*, 315–330.

Butt, J. L., & Campbell, T. L.. (1989). The effects of information order and hypothesis-testing strategies on auditors' judgments. *Accounting, Organizations and Society*, *14*, 471–480.

Carlson, E. D. (1983). An approach for designing decision support systems. In W. C. House (Ed.), *Decision Support Systems* (pp. 125-155). New York: Petrocelli Books, Inc.

Camerer, C. F. (1987). Do biases in probability judgment matter in markets: Experimental evidence. *American Economic Review*, *77*, 981–997.

Camerer, C. F. (1988). *Behavioral game theory*. Unpublished manuscript, The Wharton School, University of Pennsylvania, Philadephia.

Camerer, C. F., Loewenstein, G., & Weber, M. (1989). The curse of knowledge in economic settings: An experimental analysis. *Journal of Political Economy*, *97*, 1232–1254.

Camerer, C. F., & Weigelt, K., (1988). Experimental tests of a sequential equilibrium reputation model. *Econometrica*, *56*, 1–36.

Campbell, D. T., & Stanley, J. C. (1963). *Experimental and quasi-experimental designs for research*. Chicago: Rand-McNally.

Carlson, E. D. (1983). An approach for designing decision support systems. In W. C. House (Ed.), *Decision support systems* (pp. 125–155). New York: Petrocelli Books, Inc.

Cheng, P., & Holyoak, K. (1985). Pragmatic reasoning schemas. *Cognitive Psychology*, *17*, 391–416.

Cheng, P., Holyoak, K., Nisbett, R., & Oliver, L. (1986). Pragmatic versus syntactic approaches to training deductive reasoning. *Cognitive Psychology*, *18*, 293–328.

Chow, C. W. (1983). The effects of job standard tightness and compensation scheme on performance: An exploration of linkages. *The Accounting Review*, *58*, 667–685.

Chow, C. W., Cooper, J. C., & Waller, W. S. (1988). Participative budgeting: Effects of a truth-inducing pay scheme and information asymmetry on slack and performance. *The Accounting Review*, *63*, 111–122.

Christ, M. (1988). Attention and encoding during audit planning: An experimental study using a schematic framework. (Doctoral dissertation, University of Texas at Austin). *Dissertation Abstracts International*, *49*, 3414A.

Church, B. (1990). Auditors' use of confirmatory processes. *Journal of Accounting Literature*, *9*, 81–112

Coase, R. (1988). *The firm, the market, and the law*. Chicago: The University of Chicago Press.

Collins, A., & Loftus, E. (1975). A spreading-activation theory of semantic processing. *Psychological Review*, *82*, 407–428.

Cooper W. W., & Zeff, S. A. (1987). *Kinney's design for accounting research*. Unpublished manuscript, The University of Texas at Austin.

Corless, J. C., (1972). Assessing prior distributions for applying Bayesian statistics in auditing. *The Accounting Review*, *47*, 556–566.

Cox, J., & Isaac, R. M. (1986). Experimental economics and experimental psychology: Ever the twain shall meet? In A. MacFoyden and H. MacFoyden (Eds.), *Economic psychology: Interactions in theory and applications* (pp. 647–659). New York: Elsevier.

Cox, J., Roberson, B., & Smith, V. (1982). Theory and behavior of single object auctions. In *Research in Experimental Economics*, *2*, Greenwich, CT: JAI Press.

Crane, R. (1989, Oct. 9). Irreconcilable differences undo the 'Done Deal.' *Accounting Today*, pp. 1, 42.

Crosby, M. A. (1981). Bayesian statistics in auditing: A comparison of probability elicitation techniques. *The Accounting Review*, *56*, 355–365.

Cushing, B. E., & Loebbecke, J. K. (1984, Summer). The implications of structured audit methodologies. *The Auditor's Report*, *8*, pp. 1, 10, 13.

Cushing, B. E., & Loebbecke, J. K. (1986). *A comparison of audit methodologies of large accounting firms* (Studies in Accounting Research No. 26). Sarasota, FL: American Accounting Association.

Davis, J. (1989). *Auditor bidding behavior and independence: A laboratory markets investigation*. Unpublished manuscript, University of Illinois, Champaign.

Davis, J., & Solomon, I. (1989). Experience, expertise, and expert-performance research in public accounting. *Journal of Accounting Literature, 8*, 150–164.

Davis, J., & Swenson, C. (1988–1989). The role of experimental economics in tax policy research. *The Journal of American Taxation Association, 10*, 40–59.

DeAngelo, L. (1981). Auditor independence, 'low balling,' and disclosure regulation. *Journal of Accounting and Economics, 3*, 113–127.

DeJong, D. V., Forsythe, R., & Lundholm., R. J. (1985). Ripoffs, lemons, and reputation formation in agency relationships: A laboratory market study. *Journal of Finance, 40*, 809–820.

DeJong, D. V., Forsythe, R., & Uecker, W. C. (1985a). The methodology of laboratory markets and its implications from agency research in accounting and auditing. *Journal of Accounting Research, 23*, 753–793.

DeJong, D. V., Forsythe, R., & Uecker, W. C. (1985b, December). The relevance of laboratory markets for examining policy issues in the market for audit services. *The Accounting Forum*, pp. 27–41.

DeJong, D. V., Forsythe, R., Lundholm, R. J., & Uecker, W. C. (1985). A laboratory investigation of the moral hazard problem in agency relationships. *Journal of Accounting Research, 23*, S81–120.

Dickhaut, J. W., & Lere, J. C. (1983). Comparison of accounting systems and heuristic in selecting economic optima. *Journal of Accounting Research, 21*, 495–513.

Dillard, J. F., Kauffman, N. L., & Spires, E. E. (1989). *Evidence order and belief revision in management accounting decisions*. Unpublished manuscript, The Ohio State University, Columbus.

Dopuch, N. (1990). The auto- and cross-sectional correlations of accounting research. In T. J. Frecka (Ed.), *The state of accounting research as we enter the 1990s*. Champaign: University of Illinois.

Dopuch, N., & King, R. (1990). *Experimental tests of auditing as a credibility generating mechanism.* Unpublished manuscript, Washington University, St. Louis.

Dopuch, N., King, R., & Wallin, D. (1989). The use of experimental markets in auditing research: Some initial findings. *Auditing: A Journal of Practice and Theory*, *9*(Suppl.), 98–127.

Dow Jones & Co., Inc. (1973–1977). *Wall street journal index.* New York: Author.

Dowie, J., & Elstein, A. (1988). *Professional judgment: A reader in clinical decision making.* Cambridge, England: Cambridge University Press.

Duh, R. R., & Sunder, S. (1986). Incentives, learning and processing of information in a market environment: An examination of the base-rate fallacy. In S. Moriarty (Ed.), *Laboratory market research.* (pp. 50-79). Norman: University of Oklahoma, Center for Economic and Management Research.

Dye, R. (1985). Disclosure of nonproprietary information. *Journal of Accounting Research*, *23*, 123–145.

Edwards, W. (1968). Conservatism in human information processing. In B. Kleinmuntz (Ed.), *Formal representations of human judgment.* New York: Wiley.

Eger, C., & Dickhaut, J. (1982). An examination of the conservative information processing bias in an accounting framework. *Journal of Accounting Research*, *20*, 711–723.

Einhorn, H. (1976). A synthesis: Accounting and behavioral science. *Journal of Accounting Research*, *14*(Suppl.), 196–206.

Einhorn, H., & Hogarth, R. (1981). Behavioral decision theory: Processes of judgment and choice. *Annual Review of Psychology*, *32*, 53–88.

Einhorn, H., & Hogarth, R. (1985). *A contrast/surprise model for updating beliefs.* Unpublished manuscript, University of Chicago, Chicago.

Elliott, R. K., & Kielich, J. A. (1985, Sept.). Expert systems for accountants. *Journal of Accountancy*, *160*, 126–134.

Emby, C., & Gibbins, M. (1988). Good judgment in public accounting: Quality and justification. *Contemporary Accounting Research, 4*, 287-313.

Felix, W. L., Jr. (1976). Evidence on alternative means for assessing prior probability distributions for audit decision making. *The Accounting Review, 51*, 800-807.

Felix, W. L., Jr., & Kinney, W. R., Jr. (1982). Research in the auditor's opinion formulation process: State of the art. *The Accounting Review, 57*, 245-271.

Fiedler, K. (1982). Causal schemata: Review and criticism of a popular construct. *Journal of Personality and Social Psychology, 42*, 1001-1013.

File, R. G. (1981). Auditor prediction of client firm failure (Doctoral dissertation, The University of Texas at Austin). *Dissertation Abstracts International, 42*, 1220A.

Finn, D. W., Munter, P., & McCaslin, T. (1988). *An empirical investigation into factors affecting professional conflict in public accounting*. Unpublished manuscript.

Fisher, J. (1987). The allocation mechanism of audits: An experimental approach (Doctoral dissertation, The Ohio State University). *Dissertation Abstracts International, 48*, 688A.

Fisher, M. (1987). *The effects of reporting auditor materiality levels publicly, privately, or not at all in an experimental setting*. Paper presented at the University of Waterloo Auditing Symposium, Waterloo, Ontario, Canada.

Fisher, R. A. (1955). Statistical methods and scientific induction. *Journal of the Royal Statistical Society, Series B, (17)*, cited in: Cooper, W. W., & Zeff, S. A. (1987). *Kinney's design for accounting research*. Unpublished manuscript, University of Texas at Austin.

Forsythe, R. (1986). The application of laboratory methods to testing theories of resource allocation under uncertainty. In B. Gilad and S. Kaish (Eds.), *The handbook of behavioral economics, A*, 19-60.

Forsythe, R., Isaac, R., & Palfrey, T. (1989). Theories and tests of 'blind bidding' in sealed bid auctions. *Rand Journal of Economics*, *20*, 214–238.

Francis, J. R. (1984). The effect of audit firm size on audit prices: A study of the Australian market. *Journal of Accounting and Economics*, 6, 133–151.

Frederick, D. (1986). Auditors' representation and retrieval of knowledge in internal control evaluation. (Doctoral dissertation, University of Michigan). *Dissertation Abstracts International*, *49*, 969A.

Frederick, D., & Libby, R. (1986). Expertise and auditors' judgments of conjunctive events. *Journal of Accounting Research*, *24*, 270–290.

Gibbins, M. (1984). Propositions about the psychology of professional judgment in public accounting. *Journal of Accounting Research*, *22*, 103–125.

Gibbins, M., & Emby, C. (1985). *Evidence of the nature of professional judgment in public accounting*. Presented at the Fifth Symposium on Audit Research, University of Illinois, Champaign.

Gibbins, M., & Mason, A. (1988). *Professional judgment in financial reporting*. Toronto: Canadian Institute of Chartered Accountants.

Glaser, R. (1984). Education and thinking: The role of knowledge. *American Psychologist*, *39*, 93–104.

Gordon, L. A., & Miller, D. (1976). A contingency framework for the design of accounting information systems. *Accounting, Organizations, & Society*, *1*, 56–69.

Grease, C. E. (1984). Accounting for change. *World*, *18*, 16–17.

Grether, D. (1980). Bayes rule as a descriptive model: The representativeness bias. *Quarterly Journal of Economics*, *95*, 537–557.

Grether, D. M., & Plott, C. R. (1979). Economic theory of choice and the preference reversal phenomenon. *American Economic Review*, *69*, 623–638.

Grossman, S. (1981). The informational role of warranties and private disclosure about product quality. *Journal of Law and Economics, 24*, 461–483.

Gwilliam, D., & Macve, R. (1988, April). *The future of the audit: U.K. and U.S. auditing research*. Paper presented at the Research Conference on 'Auditing and the Future,' Edinburgh, Scotland.

Hackenbrack, K. (1989). *Assessing a company's exposure to fraudulent financial reporting: Implications of seemingly irrelevant evidence*. Unpublished manuscript, Fisher School of Accounting, University of Florida, Gainesville.

Hansen, J. V., & Messier, W. F., Jr. (1986). A preliminary test of EDP-expert. *Auditing: A Journal of Practice and Theory, 6*, 109–123.

Haskins, M. E. (1987). Client control environments: An examination of auditors' perceptions. *The Accounting Review, 62*, 542–563.

Hays, W. S. (1973). *Statistics for the social sciences*. New York: Holt, Rinehart and Winston.

Heiman, V. B. (1989). *Auditors' assessments of the strength of analytical review explanations*. Unpublished manuscript, University of Pittsburgh.

Heiman, V. B. (1990). Auditors' assessments of the likelihood of error explanations in analytical review. *The Accounting Review, 65*, 875–890

Helleloid, R.T. (1987–1988). Hindsight judgments about taxpayers' expectations. *Journal of the American Taxation Association, 9* (2), 31–46.

Hilton, R. W. (1980). Integrating normative and descriptive theories of information processing. *Journal of Accounting Research, 18*, 477–505.

Hilton, R. W., Swieringa, R. J., & Turner, M. J. (1988). Product pricing, accounting costs and use of product-costing systems. *The Accounting Review, 63*, 195–218.

Hirst, D. E., Joyce, E. J., & Schadewald, M. S. (1988). *Principles of mental accounting*. Unpublished manuscript.

Hogarth, R., & Einhorn, H. (1990). *Order effects in belief updating: The belief-adjustment model.* Unpublished manuscript, University of Chicago.

Holland, J., Holyoak, K., Nisbett, R., & Thagard, P. (1986). *Induction: Processes of inference, learning and discovery.* Cambridge, MA: MIT Press.

Holstrum, G. L., Mock, T. J., & West, R. N. (1987). *Audit evidence in the year 2000: The impact of technological change on auditing.* Available from The Institute of Internal Auditors, Altamonte Springs, FL.

Holyoak, R., & Nisbett, R. (1988). Induction. In R. Sternberg & E. Smith (Eds.), *The Psychology of human thought.* (pp. 50–91). Cambridge, England: Cambridge University Press.

Jacoby, J., Troutman, T., Kuss, A., & Mazursky, D. (1984). Experience and expertise in complex decision making. *Advances in Consumer Research, 10,* 469–472.

Jensen, M. C., & Meckling, W. H. (1976). Theory of the firm: Managerial behavior, agency costs and ownership structure. *Journal of Financial Economics, 3,* 305–360.

Jiambalvo, J., & Waller, W. (1984). Decomposition and assessments of audit risk. *Auditing: A Journal of Practice and Theory, 3,* 80–88.

Joyce, E. J. (1976). Expert judgment in audit program planning. *Journal of Accounting Research, 14*(Suppl.), 29–60.

Joyce, E. J., & Biddle, G. C. (1981a). Anchoring and adjustment in probabilistic inference in auditing. *Journal of Accounting Research, 19,* 120–145.

Joyce, E. J., & Biddle, G. C. (1981b). Are auditors' judgments sufficiently regressive? *Journal of Accounting Research, 19,* 323–349.

Jung, W., & Kwon, Y. (1988). Disclosure when the market is unsure of information endowment of mangers. *Journal of Accounting Research, 26,* 146–153.

Kachelmeier, S. J. (1990). A laboratory market investigation of the demand for auditing in an environment of moral hazard. Unpublished manuscript, University of Texas at Austin.

Kachelmeier, S. J., & Messier, W. F. (1990). An investigation of the influence of a nonstatistical decision aid on auditor sample size decisions. *The Accounting Review*, *65*, 209–226.

Keen, P. G. W., & Scott-Morton, M. S. (1978). *Decision support systems: An organizational perspective*. Reading, MA: Addison-Wesley.

Keith, J. R. (1985). *Expert systems in auditing: A practitioner's perspective*. Paper presented at the 1985 Price Waterhouse Auditing Symposium, Lake Tahoe, CA

Kelley, H. (1973). The process of causal attribution. *American Psychologist*, *28*, 107–28.

Kennedy, H. A. (1975). A behavioral study of the usefulness of four financial ratios. *Journal of Accounting Research*, *13*, 97–116.

Kida, T. (1984a). The effect of causality and speficity on data use. *Journal of Accounting Research*, *22*, 145–152.

Kida, T. (1984b). The impact of hypothesis-testing strategies on auditor use of judgment data. *Journal of Accounting Research*, *22*, 332–340.

King, R., & Wallin, D. (1991). Voluntary disclosures when seller's level of information is unknown. *Journal of Accounting Research*, *29*, 96–108.

Kinney, W. R., Jr. (1975). A decision theory approach to the sampling problem in auditing. *Journal of Accounting Research*, *13*, 117–132.

Kinney, W. R., Jr. (1986). Audit technology and preferences for auditing standards. *Journal of Accounting and Economics*, 2, 73–89.

Kinney, W. R., Jr., & Uecker, W. C. (1982). Mitigating the consequences of anchoring in auditor judgment. *The Accounting Review*, *57*, 55–69.

Knapp, M. C. (1988). *An empirical investigation of factors that audit committees use as surrogates for audit quality*. Unpublished manuscript, University of Oklahoma, Norman.

Knechel, W. R., & Messier, W. F., Jr. (1990). Sequential auditor decision making: information search and evidence evaluation. *Contemporary Accounting Research*, *6*, 386–406.

Knetsch, J. L., & Sinden, J. A. (1987). The persistence of evaluation disparities. *Quarterly Journal of Economics*, *102*, 691–695.

Knetsch, J. L., Thaler, R. H., & Kahneman, D. (1989). *Experimental tests of the endowment effect and the Coase theorem*. Unpublished manuscript.

Koch, B. S., Pei, B. K., & Reed, S. A. (1989). *Auditor belief revisions in a performance auditing setting: An application of the belief-adjustment model*. Unpublished manuscript, Arizona State University, Tempe.

Koonce, L. (1990). *Belief perseverance in audit analytical review*. Unpublished manuscript, University of Texas at Austin.

KPMG Peat, Marwick. (1987). *Audit Manual-US*. New York: Author.

Kraft, W. H., Jr. (1968). Statistical sampling for auditing: A new look. *Journal of Accountancy*, 126 (2), 49–56.

Lakatos, I. (1978). The methodology of scientific research programmes. In J. Worrall and G. Currie (Eds.), *Philosophical papers*, *1*, Cambridge, England: Cambridge University Press.

Langlois, R. (1986). *Economics as a process*. Cambridge, England: Cambridge University Press.

Lau, A. H. L. (1987). A five state financial distress prediction model. *Journal of Accounting Research*, 25, 127–138.

Lewis, B., Patton. J., & Green. S. (1988). The effects of information choice and information use on analysts' predictions of municipal bond rating changes. *The Accounting Review*, *63*, 270–282.

Libby, R. (1975). Accounting ratios and the prediction of failure: Some behavioral evidence. *Journal of Accounting Research*, *13*, 150–161.

Libby, R. (1981). *Accounting and human information processing: Theory and applications*. Englewood Cliffs, NJ: Prentice-Hall.

Libby, R. (1985). Availability and the generation of hypotheses in analytical review. *Journal of Accounting Research, 23*, 648–667.

Libby, R. (1989). *Experimental research and the distinctive features of accounting settings*. Unpublished manuscript, Cornell University, Ithaca, NY.

Libby, R., & Frederick, D. (1988). *Expertise and the ability to explain audit findings*. Unpublished manuscript, Cornell University, Ithaca, NY.

Libby, R., & Frederick, D. (1990). Experience and ability to explain audit findings. *Journal of Accounting Research, 28*, 348–367.

Libby, R., & Lewis, B. (1982). Human information processing research in accounting: The state of the art in 1982. *Accounting, Organizations, and Society, 7*, 231–286.

Libby, R., & Libby, P. (1989). Expert measurement and mechanical combination in control reliance decisions. *The Accounting Review, 64*, 729–747.

Libby, R., & Trotman, K. (1989). *Audit review as a control for biased recall of evidence in decision making*. Unpublished manuscript, Cornell University, Ithaca, NY.

Lichtenstein, S., & Fischhoff, B. (1977). Do those who know more also know more about how much they know? *Organizational Behavior and Human Performance, 20*, 159–183.

Lichtenstein, S., Fischhoff, B. & Phillips, L. D. (1982). Calibration of probabilities: State of the art to 1980. In D. Kahneman, P. Slovic, & A. Tversky (Eds.), *Judgment under uncertainty: Heuristics and biases* (pp. 306–334). Cambridge, England: Cambridge University Press.

Lopes, L. L. (1982). *Toward a procedural theory of judgment*. Unpublished manuscript, University of Wisconsin, Madison.

Lothian, N. (1983). *Audit quality and value for money: Perceptions of company financial management*. Unpublished manuscript, Heriot-Watt University, Edinburgh, Scotland.

Marchant, G. (1989). Analogical reasoning and hypothesis generation in auditing. *The Accounting Review, 64*, 500–513.

Matsumura, E. M., & Tucker, R. (1989). *Fraud detection*. Unpublished manuscript, University of Wisconsin, Madison.

McDaniel, L. (1988). The effects of time pressure and audit program structure on audit effectiveness and efficiency. (Doctoral dissertation, University of Michigan). *Dissertations Abstract International, 49*, 1192A.

Mehle, T., Gettys, C., Manning, C., Baca, S., & Fisher, S. (1981). The availability explanation of excessive plausibility assessments. *Acta Psychologica, 49*, 127–140.

Meixner, W. F., & Welker, R. B. (1988). Judgment consensus and auditor experience: An examination of organizational relations. *The Accounting Review, 63*, 505–513.

Messier, W. F., Jr. (1990). *The sequencing of audit evidence: Its impact on the extent of audit testing and report formulation*. Unpublished manuscript, Fisher School of Accounting, University of Florida, Gainesville.

Messier, W. F., Jr., & Hansen, J. V. (1984). Expert systems in accounting and auditing: A framework and review. In S. Moriarity & E. Joyce (Eds.), *Decision making and accounting: Current research* (pp. 182–202). Norman: University of Oklahoma.

Messier, W. F., Jr., & Tubbs, R. M. (1989). *Mitigating recency effects in belief revision: The impact of experience and review*. Unpublished manuscript, Fisher School of Accounting, University of Florida, Gainesville.

Milgrom, P. (1981a). An axiomatic characterization of common knowledge. *Econometrica, 49*, 219–222.

Milgrom, P. (1981b). Good news and bad news: Representation theorems and applications. *Bell Journal of Economics, 12*, 380–391.

Milliron, V. (1985). A behavioral study of the meaning and influence of tax complexity. *Journal of Accounting Research, 23*, 794–816.

Moeckel, C. (1990). The nature of auditors' memory errors during the opinion formulation process. *Journal of Accounting Research, 28*, 368–387.

Moeckel, C., & Plumlee, D. (1989). Auditors' confidence in recognition of audit evidence. *The Accounting Review, 64*, 653–666.

Moizer, P. (1988). *Audit quality: The auditor's choice*. Unpublished manuscript, Department of Accounting and Finance, University of Manchester, England.

Moser, D. V. (1989). The effects of interference, availability, and accounting information on investors' predictive judgments. *The Accounting Review, 64*, 433–448.

Newton, J. D., & Ashton, R. H. (1988, Oct. 15). *The association between audit technology and audit delay*. Presented at the Eighth Symposium on Audit Research, University of Illinois, Champaign.

Osharow, H. R. (1986). Discussant's response to "On the economics of product differentiation in auditing." In R. P. Srivastava & N. A. Fordo (Eds.), *Auditing Symposium VIII, Proceedings of the 1986 Touche Ross University of Kansas Symposium on Auditing Problems, 8*, 100–104.

Oskamp, S. (1962). The relation pf clinical experience and training methods to several criteria of clinical predictions. *Psychological Monographs. 76*.

Parsons, T. (1968). Professions. In D. L. Sills (Ed.), *The international encyclopedia of the social sciences 24*, 12 (pp. 536–547). New York: Macmillan.

Pasewark, W. R., Shockley, R. A., & Wilkerson, J. E., Jr. (1989). *An empirical investigation of auditor objectivity in normal audit settings*. Unpublished manuscript, University of Georgia, Athens.

Plumlee, R. D. (1985). The standard of objectivity for internal auditors: Memory and bias effects. *Journal of Accounting Research, 23*, 683–699.

Pound, G. D., & Francis, J. R. (1981). The accounting services market: Theory and evidence. *Journal of Business, Finance & Accounting, 8*, 353–371.

Roth, A. E. (1986). Laboratory experimentation in economics. *Economics and Philosophy, 2*, 245–273.

Rousseau, D. M., & Cooke, R. A. (1984). Technology and structure: The concrete, abstract, and activity systems of organizations. *Journal of Management, 10*, 345–364.

Sandlin, P. (1987). The effect of causal background on auditors' analytical review judgments. (Doctoral dissertation, University of Texas at Austin). *Dissertation Abstracts International, 48*, 1255A.

Schandl, C. W. (1978). *Theory of auditing*. Lawrence, KS: Scholars Book Co.

Schatzberg, J. (1990). A laboratory market investigation of low balling in audit pricing. *The Accounting Review, 65*, 339–362.

Scott, W. R. (1984). The state of the art of academic research in auditing. *Journal of Accounting Literature, 3*, 153–193.

Selto, F., & Cooper, J. (1990). *Control of risk attitude in experimental accounting research*. Unpublished manuscript, University of Colorado, Boulder.

Shibano, T. (1990). *Assessing audit risk from errors and irregularities*. Unpublished manuscript, University of California, Berkeley.

Shields, M. D. (1984). A predecisional approach to the measurement of the demand for information in a performance report. *Accounting, Organizations, and Society, 9*, 355–364.

Shiller R. (1984). Stock prices and social dynamics. In *Brookings Papers on Economic Activity No.2* (pp. 457–498). Washington: Brookings.

Simon, H. (1960). *The new science of management*. New York: Harper.

Simunic, D. A., & Stein, M. (1986). On the economics of product differentiation in auditing. In R. P. Srivastava & N. A. Fordo (Eds.), *Auditing Symposium VIII, Proceedings of the 1986 Touche Ross University of Kansas Symposium on Auditing Problems, 8*, 69–99.

Simunic, D. A., & Stein, M. (1987). *Product differentiation in auditing: Auditor choice in the market for unseasoned new issues*. Vancouver, BC, Canada: The Canadian Certified General Accountants' Research Foundation.

Slovic, P., & Lichtenstein, S. (1971). Comparison of Bayesian and regression approaches to the study of information processing in judgment. *Organization Behavior and Human Performance, 6*, 649–744.

Smith, V. (1982). Microeconomic systems as an experimental science. *American Economic Review, 72*, 923–955.

Smith, V. (1989). Theory, experiment and economics. *Journal of Economic Perspectives, 3*, 151–169.

Smith, V., Schatzberg J., & Waller, W. (1987). Experimental economics and auditing. *Auditing: A Journal of Practice and Theory, 7*, 71–93.

Solomon, I. (1982). Probability assessment by individual auditors and audit teams: An empirical investigation. *Journal of Accounting Research, 20*, 689–710.

Solomon, I. (1987). Multi-auditor judgment/decision making research. *Journal of Accounting Literature, 6*, 1–25.

Solomon, I., Ariyo, A., & Tomassini, L. A. (1985). Contextual effects on the calibration of probabilistic judgments. *Journal of Applied Psychology, 70*, 528–532.

Solomon, I, Krogstad, J. L., Romney, M. B., & Tomassini, L. A. (1982). Auditing prior probability distributions for account balances. *Accounting, Organizations, and Society, 7*, 27–41.

Solomon, I., Tomassini, L. A., Romney, M. B., & Krogstad, J. L. (1984). Probability elicitation in auditing: Additional evidence on the equivalent prior sample method. *Advances in Accounting, 1*, 267–290.

Sommer, A. A., Jr. (1989). The challenge of the mergers. *Accounting Horizons, 3*, 103–106.

Sorter, G. H. (1969). An 'events' approach to basic accounting theory. *The Accounting Review, 44*, 12–19.

Taylor, S., & Fiske, S. (1978). Salience, attention and attribution: Top of the head phenomena. In L. Berkowitz (Ed.), *Advances in experimental social psychology, 11* (pp. 249–88). New York: Academic Press.

Tetlock, P. E. (1983). Accountability and the perseverance of first impressions. *Social Psychology Quarterly, 46*, 285–292.

Thaler, R. (1980). Toward a positive theory of consumer choice. *Journal of Economic Behavior and Organization, 1*, 39–60.

Thaler, R. (1986). The psychology and economics conference handbook: Comments on Simon, on Einhorn and Hogarth, and on Tversky and Kahneman. *Journal of Business, 59*, S279–S284.

Thaler, R. (1987). The psychology of choice and assumptions of economics. In A. E. Roth (Ed.), *Laboratory experimentation in economics*. (pp. 234–255). Cambridge, England: Cambridge University Press.

To merge or not to merge, that is the question. (1977, Dec. 1). *Forbes*, 58–59.

Tomassini, L. A., Solomon, I, Romney, M. B., & Krogstad, J. L. (1982). Calibration of auditors' probabilistic judgments: Some empirical evidence. *Organizational Behavior and Human Performance, 29*, 391–406.

Topalian, A. (1984). Corporate identity: Beyond the visual overstatements. *International Journal of Advertising, 3*, 55–62.

Trotman, K. (1983). Individual and group judgments of internal control systems. *Journal of Accounting Research, 21*, 234–255.

Trotman, K. (1985). The review process and the accuracy of auditor judgments. *Journal of Accounting Research, 23*, 740–752.

Trotman K., & Yetton, P. (1985). The effect of the review process on auditor judgments. *Journal of Accounting Research, 23*, 256–267.

Tubbs, R. M., Messier, W. F., Jr., & Knechel, W. R. (1990). Recency effects in the auditor's belief revision process. *The Accounting Review, 65*, 452–460.

Tversky, A., & Kahneman, D. (1974). Judgment under uncertainty: Heuristics and biases. *Science, 185*, 1124–1131.

Tversky, A., & Kahneman, D. (1982a). Availability: A heuristic for judging frequency and probability. In D. Kahneman, P. Slovic, & A. Tversky (Eds.), *Judgment under uncertainty: Heuristics and biases* (pp. 163–178). Cambridge, England: Cambridge University Press.

Tversky, A., & Kahneman, D. (1982b). Judgments of and by representativeness. In D. Kahneman, P. Slovic, & A. Tversky (Eds.), *Judgment under uncertainty: Heuristics and biases* (pp. 84–100). Cambridge, England: Cambridge University Press.

Tversky, A., & Kahneman. D. (1986). Rational choice and the framing of decisions. *Journal of Business, 59*, S251–S278.

Uecker, W. C. (1982). The quality of group performance in simplified information evaluation. *Journal of Accounting Research, 20*, 388–402.

Uecker, W., & Kinney, W. (1977). Judgmental evaluation of sample results: A study of the type and severity of errors made by practicing CPA's. *Accounting, Organizations, and Society, 3*, 269–275.

Walker, J., Smith V., & Cox, J. (1989). *Inducing risk neutral preferences: An examination in a controlled market environment.* Unpublished manuscript, University of Arizona, Tucson.

Wallace, J. J., & Wallace, W. A., (1990, May). Learning from peer review comments. *The CPA Journal*, 48–53.

Wallace, W. A. (1986). *Auditing*. New York: Macmillan.

Wallace, W. A. (1987). The economic role of the audit in free and regulated markets: A review. *Research in Accounting Regulation, 1*, 7–34.

Wallace, W. A. (1988). *The content of peer review public files.* Unpublished manuscript, Texas A&M University, College Station.

Wallace, W. A. (1991). *Auditing*. Boston: Kent.

Waller, W. S., & Chow, C. W. (1985). The self-selection and effort effects of standard-based employee contracts: A framework and some empirical evidence. *The Accounting Review, 60*, 458–476.

Waller, W. S, & Felix, W. L., Jr. (1984a). The auditor and learning from experience: Some conjectures. *Accounting, Organizations, and Society*, *12*, 383–406.

Waller, W. S., & Felix, W. L., Jr. (1984b). The effects of incomplete outcome feedback on auditors' self-perceptions of judgment ability. *The Accounting Review*, *59*, 637–646.

Waller, W. S., & Felix, W. L., Jr. (1987). Auditors' covariation judgments. *The Accounting Review*, *62*, 275–292.

Waller, W. S., & Felix, W. L. Jr. (1989). Auditors' causal judgments: Effects of forward versus backward inference on information processing. *Accounting, Organizations, and Society*, *14*, 179–200.

Wallin, D., (1989). Alternative economic institutions to motivate managerial disclosure of private information: An experimental markets examination (Doctoral dissertation, University of Arizona).

Weber, R. (1980). Some characteristics of the free recall of computer controls by EDP auditors. *Journal of Accounting Research*, *18*, 214–241.

Wilde, L. (1980). On the use of laboratory experiments in economics. In J. Pitt (Ed.), *The philosophy of economics*, (pp. 137–148). Norwell, MA: Reidel.

Williams, A. (1980). Computerized double auction markets: Some initial experimental results. *The Journal of Business*, *53*, 235–258.

Williams, D. D., & Dirsmith, M. W. (1987). *The effects of audit technology on auditor efficiency: Auditing and the timeliness of client earnings announcements*. Unpublished manuscript.

Williamson, O. (1975). *Markets and hierarchies: Analysis and antitrust implications*. New York: Macmillan.

Williamson, O. (1985). *The economic institutions of capitalism: Firms markets, relational contracting*. New York: Free Press.

Wright, W. F. (1988). Judgment consensus and experience. In K. R. Ferris (Ed.), *Behavioral accounting research: A critical analysis*. (pp. 305–328). Columbus: Publishing Horizons.

Zavgren, C. V. (1983). The prediction of corporate failure: The state of the art. *Journal of Accounting Literature*, 2, 1–38.

Zmijewski, M. E. (1984). Methodological issues related to the estimation of financial distress prediction models. *Journal of Accounting Research*, 22(Suppl.), 59–82.